In Search Of BURMA

In Search Of BURMA

by Caroline Courtauld
Introduction by Professor Hugh Tinker

Frederick Muller Limited
London

First published in Great Britain in 1984 by
Frederick Muller Limited, London SW19 7JZ

Copyright © Caroline Courtauld 1984

Designed and produced by Odyssey Productions Ltd.

Printed in Hong Kong by South China Printing Co.

Preceding picture *Rising from the water of the Inle Lake is Phaung
Daw Pagoda, one of the three principal shrines in Burma.*

A gold spire of the Kyauktan Pagoda glistens against the dappled midday sky. Also called Ye Le Paya (In the middle of water) this pagoda is only accessible by boat. Some thirteen miles away is Syriam, a town with a bizarre history. In 1600 when it was a thriving seaport and the southern outpost of the Arakanese Kingdom, Felipe de Brito, a Portuguese and formerly a member of the king's body-guard, was appointed Governor. He immediately fortified the city, placed it under Portuguese sovereignty and for the next thirteen years ruled as self-declared "King of Lower Burma".

Contents

A seasoned pwe enthusiast lights her cigar. The Burmese are a nation of smokers from nearly the smallest ("Burmese children never smoke before they can walk") to the oldest grandmother.

Once a year during the full
moon of Tawthalin (August /
September) this magnificent
copy of a royal Karaweik barge
shaped like a golden swan
(symbol of Buddhist royalty),
conveys four of the five gold
Buddha images, from their home
in the Phaung Daw U Pagoda,
around the Inle Lake to visit
neighbouring pagodas.

Preface

One hot August day in 1976 my family and I arrived to live in Singapore. High-rise, clean, efficient, admirable — rather than the East I had imagined, here was "instant Asia". In search of a more authentic Orient I happened upon Burma. My instinct, I discovered later, was just what Kipling's had been, "this is Burma, and it will be quite unlike any land you know about". Then, as if in confirmation, "a golden mystery upheaved itself on the horizon": I had glimpsed the Shwedagon Pagoda for the first time. The spell was cast and many subsequent visits have strengthened its hold.

A definitive work on Burma, its history, society and culture would have been far beyond me. Instead I have assembled a pot-pourri of fable, folklore and customs; religion, anecdote and threads of history. From these ingredients and drawing extensively on observations and experiences of previous travellers in Burma as well as my own, I have tried in words and pictures to distil the essence of my captivation for this serene and elegant land. Perhaps the potential traveller — Burma remains (but for how long?) a country for the traveller rather than the tourist — will find something in these pages to titillate his or her interest.

I could have made virtually no progress in my own attempts to discover Burma or to record the results without the support of numerous friends. In particular, Roland Vandenbossche (of Schlumberger) guided my first faltering (and many subsequent) footsteps in Burma, told me where to go, how to get there and whom to see. Kenneth Maung Maung Pa, oriental Renaissance Man, made many journeys with me, beguiled me with stories and told me about Buddha. Marcus Ba Myaing also travelled with me, provided another perspective and magically made things happen. Dr. Anil Seal of Trinity College, Cambridge, must share the blame for this volume's existence; "we must do a book", he said but, sadly for the reader, turned out to be writing too many others himself. Charles Booth, lately British Ambassador in Rangoon and accomplished Burmaphile, opened firmly bolted doors. Professor Than Nyun of Rangoon University epitomised the Middle Way. His father, U Nyun, inspired me by radiating pure Buddhism. So did U Myint Thein, poet, politician and, albeit impishly, grand old man. Magnus Bartlett, courageous

publisher, astonished me by agreeing to handle the book in the first place and cajoled and encouraged me along the way. My husband, William, reunited my infinitives and enthused about some of my pictures.

To all of these I express my warm gratitude. However, perhaps it is to the people of Burma as a whole that I am in deepest debt. For, as observed by the nineteenth-century colonial Sir George Scott, "it is their natural kindness and that first of all qualifications for the title of gentleman, consideration for the feelings of others, which make the Burmese such general favourites with all who come across them".

For centuries the Palaung hill people have collected and stored their water (and liquor) in hollowed-out bamboo — a process simplified by the advent of the village tap.

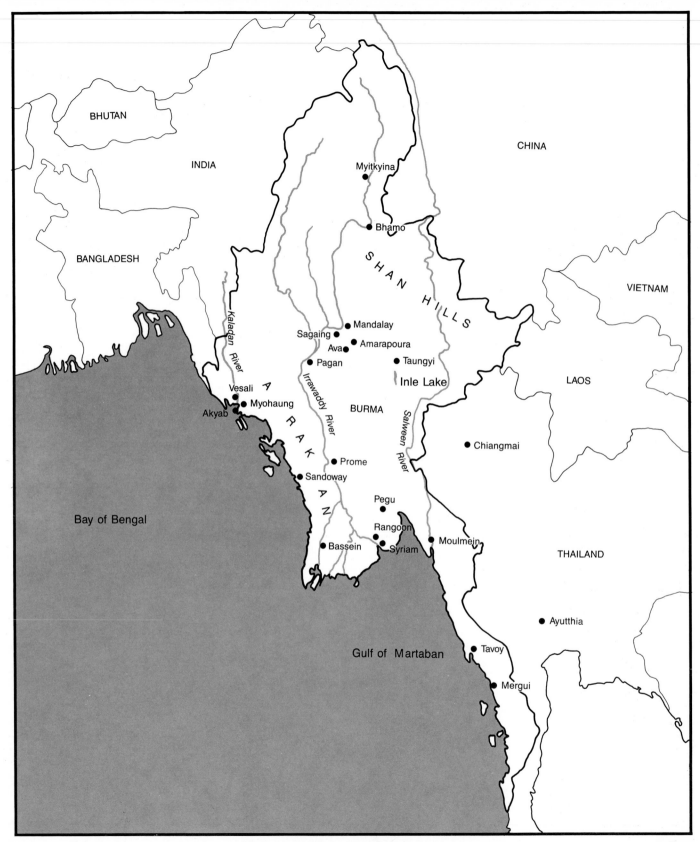

BHUTAN

INDIA

CHINA

BANGLADESH

VIETNAM

S H A N   H I L L S

Myitkyina

Bhamo

Mandalay

Sagaing

Ava

Amarapoura

Pagan

Taungyi

Inle Lake

LAOS

Vesali

Myohaung

Akyab

BURMA

Chiangmai

Prome

Sandoway

Pegu

Rangoon

Moulmein

THAILAND

Bassein

Syriam

Bay of Bengal

Ayutthia

Tavoy

Gulf of Martaban

Mergui

Kaladan River

Irrawaddy River

Salween River

A R A K A N

Contemporary Map of Burma

Introduction *by Professor Hugh Tinker*

Burma is one of the few countries where a foreign visitor is still a traveller, not a tourist. The round-the-world jumbo jets do not call at Rangoon's modest airport, Mingaladon. One must get there either by Union of Burma Airways or Thai Airways, flying in from Bangkok or Calcutta or Kathmandu. No glossy brochures advertise package tours to Burma. Of course there are foreign visitors, but they are swallowed up into the life of Burma as soon as they arrive. For a long time, the government of Burma virtually excluded all foreigners by issuing 24-hour visas only. In recent years, though, visas have been extended to a week, allowing a visitor just enough time to see the most important places described by Caroline Courtauld: the Shwedagon Pagoda, the city of Mandalay, and the ancient temple city of Pagan. The persistent foreigner who demonstrates a serious interest in some cultural feature of the Burmese life can secure an extension, once arrived in Rangoon. The Burmese are not at all unfriendly — and they do not have anything to hide. But they have not forgotten centuries of experience of foreigners who arrived with bland faces and then stayed to impose their rule on Burma: culminating in the long period of British occupation and the short but bitter Japanese domination, of which Dr. Htin Aung (the leading Burmese historian) observes: "The period of Japanese military rule lasted only three years but to the Burmese people it was more irksome than some sixty years of British Rule."

So the Burmese have not opened their land to a flood of tourists, as so many Third World states have done. For those foreigners who do get there, the reward is great. Probably, visually, Burma is unique. I know of no other land where the eye is so constantly delighted by scenes of casual, almost unintended beauty. This beauty is partly provided by landscape and flora (the botanist will discover orchids, and other flowers thought of as rare, growing casually by the wayside), while the work of man harmonises with the landscape. There are the villages raised upon stilts, structures made of bamboo and palm, as natural as nature, and above all the white and golden temples, strewn across field and mountain like a cascade of jewels.

But the chief beauty of Burma lies in its people. Like most of the races of Southeast Asia, the Burmese all look delightful. Their clothing is simple but graceful. Their faces and bodies are lithe and supple, their eyes are alight, their voices are warm. They are animated by a kind of exhilaration: each maiden is a princess, each youth a prince. In middle age, their features retain the unlined freshness of youth, and most retain their figures. Those ladies who become plump in middle age carry their extra inches with a style and a swing. Old age seems to come dramatically in Burma. A man of sixty, who a few years back still had a face like a boy, will suddenly look lined, with skin like parchment. The eyes that were sparkling are still. An old man, especially perhaps a wizened old monk, has his own kind of beauty, though not entirely of this world.

Age is highly respected in Burma. Treated with honour, almost veneration, the old have reached a happy time of life. Babyhood is a lovely time in Burma also. You do not see a crying child: if one snivels it is immediately snatched up and comforted. Babyhood tends to be extended, and it must be a traumatic experience for a boy to leave home and spend his period as a novice in a monastery, despite the excitement of the occasion which Caroline Courtauld so delicately describes.

The traveller need have no hesitation in stepping out of the hotel: no one will molest you, and no one will try to beg, except perhaps in the environs of Rangoon's main hotel for foreign businessmen. The only folk who solicit alms are emissaries from temples and monasteries, and they approach Burmese lay people as of right. These men of religion will not ask from a foreigner, who has no conception that they are bestowing merit upon the donor, not vice-versa.

The English-speaking traveller should eventually find someone able to explain things. For some twenty years the policy of the government was to downgrade the use of English (except for scientists and doctors) but recently all that has changed, and English is now taught in high schools and colleges. Anyhow, the traveller soon finds that communication somehow rises above the language medium. Few places are closed to the visitor. Anyone entering the

---

1   Maung Htin Aung, A History of Burma, Columbia, 1967, p. 301.

surroundings of a religious foundation must first remove shoes and stockings; and also be decently clad (shorts are not usual). Visitors can then wander more or less where they will. A monk or other custodian will soon warn anyone off forbidden ground; but without officiousness or assertiveness.

The attitude of Burmese to foreigners is a bit of a puzzle. Everywhere you will be met by smiling faces. Almost everywhere, people will try to help you. If you board a bus, they will find a place for you. It is very rare indeed for anyone to be rude. And yet, I have come to the conclusion that the Burmese do not really have any feeling for or against foreigners. If they are guests, they will be treated with care and courtesy. But they are really outside Burmese life and not of any consequence. Even in a remote village where no foreigner has ever been seen, if a car with white occupants should draw up, no one (not even the children) will show great curiosity: though they may laugh. Laughter can be (in Burma, as elsewhere) a way of handling an unfamiliar situation.

If you get to know an educated Burmese quite well he will probably explain that in Burmese custom an important element is the consciousness of *ana-dè*. This is an untranslatable term which crudely means ''to be ill at east'' or ''not to impose or be imposed upon''. Burmans have a strong sense of what is proper and what improper, which frequently does not coincide with that of the Westerner. It is just as well for the visitor to remember that ''East is East and West is West'', or else things can prove frustrating. Misunderstandings arise — unexpected delays, unexplained non-appearances and unexpected happenings. The Burmese response to any of these is likely to be that of laughter. The worst response is a burst of irritation or anger. This will be simply bad manners to the Burmese who will reply by being even more insouciant.

Is it all worth it then? Yes, it certainly is; and Caroline Courtauld's pictures and narrative provide ample evidence of this. She has captured the essence of Burma: which is timelessness, the approachway to deathlessness, or *Nirvana*. The roads of Rangoon may be crowded with the most modern German or Japanese cars and trucks — but beyond the city limits the bullock cart still provides the main form of transport. Water buffalo wend their ponderous way to stream

or pond. Men plough their fields with the same wooden ploughs their grandfathers employed. Women plant rice, according to ancient tradition: for other crops like beans, gourds or pulses are just grown for consumption, but rice is grown for the gods.

It is this timelessness which is the essence of Burma. The pace of life is leisurely. People stroll by; nobody runs. One is most aware of this timelessness during the festival season. Caroline Courtauld describes, very vividly, the *pwè*, the dance-drama which draws upon the traditions of the past and yet which is so contemporary in its allusions and pointed comments. The Burmese are conscious of their past infusing their present and mingling in their future; all, of course, contributing to that timelessness which will free them from the changes and chances of this transitory life and bring them to Nirvana, beyond the world, beyond time. ''Life is but a bubble on the ocean's surface'' tells a Burmese proverb. We are all travellers who set out long ago and who must wander till we reach the goal — whenever that may be. In the West we are all too conscious of ''Time's winged chariot hurrying near''. Not so the Burmese who observe, ''A man does not lose his life if the time which he is fated to die has not arrived''.

So, relax with the Burmese, as Caroline Courtauld does. Their way of life has much to teach us. We need not idealise or idolise Burma. The West has made its impact, but rather as a travelling fun-fair makes an impact on a sleepy village. Go into a hallowed, time-old shrine of the Buddha: the massive figure, withdrawn in meditation, is illuminated by dizzy neon strip lighting. The intoning of the monks is overlaid by a loudspeaker, turned up full. Here are young men and maidens, flirting lazily by the lakeside; their dalliance is hotted up from a transistor radio. Somehow, these vulgar instrusions cannot break the spell. Burma remains inviolate: the timeless East which so many Europeans and Americans have tried in vain to find.

Probably, by Western measurements, Burma is not affluent: the per capita income is somewhere between that of Paraguay and Upper Volta. Who cares? Burma is not poor in the way that India is poor: that is, on the edge of starvation and squalor. A Burmese village is simple in the extreme. The people have the most modest means. Yet almost every man

1 Hla Pe, Burmese Proverbs, John Murray, 1962.

has a clean shirt and a cigar in his mouth; and assuredly every woman has a crisp blouse and skirt which delight her and the onlooker — and she has jasmine in her hair. Each night, when they go to bed (early when the harvest must be reaped, late when it is the festival season) they sleep with a full stomach of rice. Burma does not suffer from the twin nightmares of under-production and over-population which haunt the Third World. The country could feed twice the present population; but long ago Burmese women learned how to regulate the arrival of babies to suit their circumstances.

Perhaps it is the almost unique status of Burmese women which makes the country what it is. As Caroline Courtauld explains, they achieved equality with men when this was only the dream of a few female pioneers in the West. In the commercial sphere, one gets the strong impression that it is the women who keep it all going. If Burmese men have set up the state sector of regulated trade and industry, it is the women who give vitality to the "black market" sector (the name is absurd because this supplies all the consumer goods on sale in Burma).

Along with their capability, Burmese women radiate a sweet femininity. Probably Burmese men accept the powerful role their women play because the women make their men feel good, feel important, while sweetly having their own way. Among professional people it is not at all uncommon for a wife who is a doctor or an academic to depart for two or three years to Europe or America, leaving the husband to look after the children and home.

How much of all this the one-week visitor can absorb I do not know. Certainly, this book will enlarge the vision. With great sympathy and understanding Caroline Courtauld has brought Burma to life within these pages. Accompany her to the Shwedagon temple, along the majestic Irrawaddy River, into the revels of the water festival, away to the misty backwaters of Arakan. For some, this may be a prelude to actually stepping down at Mingaladon airfield; to many just the prelude to a journey of the imagination. Either can be delightful — and unexpected - for, as the Burmese say, "I didn't know my mother-in-law was going to die! If I had, I would have bought a horse to ride."

View From the Pagoda *Author's Foreword*

"There bathed in sunshine, secret and still, was Buddhist Burma". Before the traveller can enter this Shangri-la, as if to test his credentials for sampling the mysteries that lie within, he must negotiate the bureaucratic maze that is Rangoon Airport. The jet liner of the modern world roars off leaving the bemused visitor to be slowly processed through customs and immigration. Smiling officials stand behind wooden counters. Overhead, fans slowly circulate the hot air which, as 200 people flood into the small area, rises to new heights. An hour or so later, nursing a sore hand from frenetic form filling, and sore elbows and shins from jostling for a precious spot at the counter, you emerge: suddenly the cares of the world tumble from your shoulders. It no longer matters that you are hot, tired and dirty, or you do not have the correct currency to tip the small boy wielding your bag. A confidence has crept into your being that all is well and, like Mary Lennox in *The Secret Garden*, you are through that door and there is "the sweetest, most mysterious-looking place anyone could imagine".

Jogging along the airport road into Rangoon seated in a disintegrating pre-war Buick or the like Buddhist Burma unfurls. A gentle fragrance fills the hot dusty air. Elegant men and women dressed in *longyis* go about their business. Their elders, sitting in front of their brown crisscross mat houses, survey the scene. Yellow-robed monks wander quietly along the road whilst a gang of chattering children follow on behind, endlessly tying their longyis. The landscape is dotted with multifarious pagodas and *nat* shrines (dedicated to spirit gods) nestled in spreading trees. However, the true enchantment of the country is experienced with the first glimpse of the dauntingly beautiful Shwedagon Pagoda. The golden spire towers over the city like a glittering flame, inviting all who look to make a pilgrimage up the long stairway to the marble terraces.

Rangoon is a handsome city with a history of over 2,000 years, though a capital for a mere hundred. Rebuilt on the grid system in the 1850s, the wide tree-lined boulevards are bordered by fine stone buildings. In the 1880s Rangoon was renowned as "Queen of the East" and such were her prospects, according to Sir George Scott (see Suggested Reading, page 109), that her trade would outstrip Calcutta before the end of the century and that "hitherto the progress made will compare with the most vaunted American city successes." How happily wrong he proved to be! Today Rangoon bustles without urgency, high-rise buildings, traffic jams or department stores. Instead, curious shops sell everything from antique lacquerware and silver-backed dressing table sets, left over from colonial days, to plastic buckets and second-hand Dorothy L. Sayers novels. There is no forest of television aerials to upset the roofscapes, no vast hoardings proclaiming the latest jingles of the advertising men: instead there are stylish hand-painted movie advertisements or a charming wedding portrait of the Prince and Princess of Wales to sell the skills of the Black and White Tailors.

Burma abounds in contradictions. This gentle Buddhist country has a supremely violent history and today the government forces are engaged both with communist insurgents and also with ethnic groups seeking autonomy. She also nurtures dual economies — one legal, one illegal. It is hard to walk outside a tourist hotel without a furtive whisperer inviting one to change money at the unofficial rate. The black markets themselves are no hole-in-the-corner affairs. The rows of cassette players, motor bikes and cosmetics — all smuggled across from Thailand — are displayed alongside local Shan bags, longyis and religious paraphernalia, without apparent embarrassment and only token police intervention.

The main artery of Burma is the Irrawaddy River and, since the time of the Gautama Buddha (567-487 B.C.), its banks have provided sites for the royal capitals. It was thought to be unlucky for a king to use the same capital as his predecessor, so their sites have been shuttled up and down the river like tramp steamers. At Pagan (capital from 1044 to 1287), for sixteen square miles the whole surface is thickly studded with pagodas of all shapes and sizes. Climb the tallest pagoda before dawn and watch the sun creep up behind them. In the gentle light long shadows merge dream and

This Burmese court dress, here modelled by a Karen beauty, was in vogue until the exile and dissolution of King Theebaw and Queen Supyalat's court by the British in 1886. Today it is often worn by minthani, the female dancers at a pwè.

reality; but, as the fantasies of the dawn give way to the realities of the day, the contours become clear. The great monuments stand aside from their smaller, chaotic neighbours with their grass ''hairdos'', and everywhere the red brick radiates warmth. Looking down with wonderment at this enchanted scene it is impossible to imagine it was the arena of many fierce power struggles. One of the most bizarre of these occured in 1287 when the then Burmese King Narathihapate refused to pay tribute to Kublai Khan. Instead, relates Marco Polo, ''he gathered together an army of 2,000 large elephants. On each of these was erected a wooden castle of great strength and admirably adapted for warfare. Each of these castles was manned by at least twelve fighting men. In addition he had fully 40,000 men''. Apparently the Khan's army was mesmerized by the advancing castle-adorned elephants, but having regained their equilibrium they showered arrows on the unsuspecting beasts who in turn bolted for the forest, throwing off their helpless appendages. On the return of his defeated army the King — the master of 300 concubines and the glutton of 300 curries daily — tore down numerous pagodas to fortify his city against the advancing Chinese invaders. The latter, Marco Polo would have us believe, were an army of jugglers and jesters from the Khan's court, although the Burmese chronicles disagree. Before any confrontation could take place the King fled south thus gaining the ignominious title of Tarokpyenrin: ''The King who ran away from the Chinese, leaving his capital to the invaders''.

Some 100 miles upstream from Pagan the Irrawaddy glides beneath ''the gilded spires of Mandalay and the pagoda-sprinkled heights of Sagaing''. Nearby, continued the tireless nineteenth-century chronicler Sir George Scott, above ''well foliaged banks at Ava and Amarapoura. . .more pagodas rise up in massive dignity. This sight, with the background of the huge dark Shan hills to the eastward, is striking and beautiful in the extreme''. These place with their romantic names have all hosted capitals, and the buildings they have to show today are legacies of their magnificent past. Of Burma's last great palace, the Gem City of Mandalay, little remains except the castellated outer brick walls and the 225-foot wide moat where, 140 years ago, the royal barges ''gilt from stem to stern''

manned by as many as sixty paddlers, floated amongst the lotus blossom, while behind the palace walls the most heinous crimes were perpetrated. In 1879 during a staging of a three day pwè (or entertainment for his subject) King Theebaw had murdered — noisy music helped deafen the sound of butchery — eighty of his close relatives he thought were conspiring to depose him. Enclosed in red velvet bags these royal corpses were then deposited in the Irrawaddy — red velvet to mask and absorb the blood, the sight of which horrified the Burmese.

Burma boasts a natural democracy and liberation for its womenfolk. From the lowliest origins they could spin to the top; the last Queen was the granddaughter of a fisherman. There has never been any caste system or primogeniture (absence of the latter of course fuelling palace intrigues and murders). Burmese women have for centuries enjoyed a freedom and equality only recently hankered after by their Western sisters — able to choose their own marriage partner, to remain the owner of any money brought to the union and with freedom of divorce. It is not uncommon for the woman to be the business manager whilst the man cares for the children. F. Tennyson Jesse explains the woman's role nicely: ''every Burman knows, as a good Buddhist, that a woman can never be the equal of a man, but every Burmese husband knows also that his wife is the better man of the two.''

Burma is a country of a different time where time itself moves at a different speed; a country of quiet eccentricity and most gentle charm; a country apart — but contentedly and even determinedly apart — from the world. This to me is its special appeal. But what caused this insulation if not fossilization? Burma's geographic isolation and the nature of the peoples drawn to the fruitful plains of the Irrawaddy provide some of the answers. But the real key seems to lie in the arrival and influence of Buddhism (and in particular the Theravada form) and its interaction with Burma's geographic and ethnic circumstances.

Burma is surrounded on three sides by high mountains and dense forests and on the fourth by the sea. This degree of impenetrability has meant protection from the casual visitor. The Irrawaddy valley was probably inhabited 5,000 years ago, but by whom no one is certain. But there are few, if any, documentary references to travellers visiting Burma prior to the second century B.C. In 128 B.C. the Chinese Emperor Wu Ti of the Han Dynasty sent his emissary Chang Ch'ien to Central Asia in search of new land routes to the Roman Empire. After a ten-year journey Chang Ch'ien returned to China and recommended that a route across Northern Burma be opened thus linking China to Bactria; however, the terrain made it impracticable. Nevertheless it did not prove too difficult for the Pyu and Burmese (Mramma) tribes, who in about the first century A.D. crossed from southeast Tibet in search of more fertile lands, a better climate and escape from local hostilities. At about the same time the Mons migrated from what is today Thailand, and settled in eastern Burma. Finally to the west, the kingdom of Wethali (Arakan) was invaded by the Mongols and, as a result, became a vassal state of Pagan. So by the tenth century this ethnic pot-pourri had gathered, forming their separate kingdoms within this secluded land "where the soil only requires to be scratched to bring forth abundant crops".

Then in 1058 an event took place which has shaped Burmese history and indeed the very persona of the Burmese people right down to the present day. A young monk named Shin Arahan who had travelled north from the Mon Kingdom converted King Anawrahta of Pagan to Theravada Buddhism. Anawrahta had wearied of the Tantric spirit and animal worship by which the original forms of Buddhism had been corrupted and took to the pure faith with startling zeal. Thirsting for further knowledge he appealed to the Mon King for a copy of the Theravada Buddhist scripture, Tripitika. When this was not forthcoming he massed his forces and marched on the southern capital. Returning home victorious, he brought not only the prized scriptures but also King Manuha and his entire court. With the overthrow of the Mon Kingdom, the only other powerful domain, it was the work of a few skirmishes to bring the remaining states into line, thus for the first time both uniting Burma and also giving it an official religion.

But why did Theravada Buddhism enjoy such instant success and how has it remained such a strong influence on the structure of society and development of the country? Perhaps the answer is to be found in the confluence of "Mongol" tribes that had fled their countries of origin in order to preserve their individualism, discovering in Theravada Buddhism a faith that perfectly complemented their mode of society. The equality of all men and women, the emphasis on order and discipline and disdain for the caste system of Hinduism were fundamental to its appeal. This new religion quickly buried itself deep in the consciousness of the people. Hitherto the Burmese had not had a script, so having evolved one the mammoth task of translating the Tripitaka from Pali was undertaken. Monasteries were built where children were taught to read and write and learn the scriptures, again emphasising equal opportunity. The country's insulation seems to have had an intensifying effect on Buddhism with the people becoming too caught up with their pursuit of Nirvana to be concerned with the outside world. Indeed they were cosily aware of their individuality and convinced of their superiority — ideas encouraged by the circumstance of a small population living in a land of plenty. Over the centuries the Burmese continued to be moulded by their geography and religion. As historian Dr. Htin Aung suggests, "the pattern of Burmese history became a chequerboard with black squares of insularity and white squares of 'internationalism', most of the time being spent safely on the black ones with the occasional tentative excursions on to the white."

Little has changed today. Some of the expertise the outside world has to offer is utilised but mass modernity holds little or no appeal for these mysterious beautiful people. Burma remains intensely herself.

Following picture *The serene Nga Phai Chaung Monastery exemplifies the Burmese talent for transforming the basest raw material (here corrugated iron roofing) into an object of poetry.*

Quest for Nirvana

"HOW great a favour has the Lord Buddha bestowed on me in manifesting to me his law through the observation of which I may escape hell and secure my salvation." To a Buddhist Burman the quest for Nirvana — literally the extinction of all passions and desires, which has also come to mean a state of perfect beatitude — is the pivot of life. Nirvana is the zenith of the Ladder of Existence, the Four States of Punishment, the nadir. An individual's position on the Ladder will depend on how much merit has been accrued during his previous lives. Those unfortunates doomed to the States of Punishment have to endure thousands of years in bubbling furnaces, their ever-renewing flesh being torn to shreds by odious gargoyles and five-headed dogs. The destiny of mortals who did not curb their passions and were abusive on earth is the profoundest state of hell, the *Bông* of Animals. Some animals, though, such as the hare, white elephant and pigeon, are exempt from the Bông, as they are believed to have been former incarnations of the Gautama Buddha. The vulture too is above the Bông as it does not take life but rather lives off carrion. Once having fallen into these macabre states of hell it is not at all clear how the victim climbs out; but avoiding them appears to depend on close adherence to the Five Great Precepts, while one's advance up the Ladder is a question of accruing merit.

A further dimension to this accounting system is *Karma*.
"The books say well my brothers
   each man's life
The outcome of his former living is,
The bygone wrongs bring forth sorrows and woes,
The bygone night breeds bliss."
So, if one's former life has been meritorious one is reborn not only higher up the scale but with good Karma. There is no recognised method of improving one's Karma, though some employ a *bedin-saya*, a sort of fortune-teller, to prescribe a *khamé* or charm to keep the evil influences at bay.

The collection of merit therefore is all important, as it can save the soul from the bubbling Bông of Animals and store credit for a future life. If one stops in a village hot and weary from a long motorcar journey, the villagers will provide *lapet* (a fermented tea) or their local brew such as toddy wine, hose down the tyres, offer to show one their pagoda and suggest a siesta on the cool floor of one of their houses. These gestures of hospitality are offered with such charm that the traveller is unconscious of the underlying ulterior motive — to gain merit. This search for merit is evident in practically every aspect of Burmese daily life. At one end of the scale is the placing by the roadside of clay water pots from which any thirsty traveller may refresh himself. At the other end is pagoda building ("no work of merit is so richly paid as the building of a pagoda"). Conversely and, one is inclined to feel, somewhat unfairly, the repairing of an existing pagoda, unless it happens to be one of the renowned shrines such as the Shwedagon, gains no merit for the repairer, but only for the original donor. This is surely one of the key factors underlying the astonishing profusion of pagodas with which the Burmese countryside, and in particular the plains of the Irrawaddy, are so liberally sprinkled. Of course it is only the rich man who is able to make this grand gesture. For the majority, the quest for Nirvana consists of attempting to live by the Five Great Precepts, preparing food for the monks and indulgence in premeditated acts of merit such as freeing caged birds. (One might well inquire how the catching of the birds in the first place affected the merit of those concerned.) There is even a festival for the liberation of fish. In the rainy season when the rivers rise to form flood lakes, the trapped fish are caught and kept in huge "chatties". They are later released amid much fun and frolic into the river. Unlike hunters, Burmese fishermen are not despised; after all they save the fish from drowning!

To the extent that Burma can be considered to possess a manufacturing sector, its backbone is certainly the group of cottage industries that produce "Nirvana goods". The craftsmen and apprentices of the guilds of Mandalay churn out fine Buddha images from alabaster, wood and marble. They also cast copper, silver and gold images by the lost wax process. But perhaps most idiosyncratic of all is the production of gold leaf. Gold nuggets from mines in the north of Burma are first flattened to paper thinness and then placed between layers of

From across Rangoon's Karaweik Lake the Shwedagon Pagoda "rears its lofty head in perfect splendour".

leather. In a small hut forbidden to women stand two men, a long-handled sledge hammer between their legs. For ten minutes at a time these muscular characters — reminiscent of the "Lord of the High Mountain" and his hammer of "fifty *viss*" (see p. 38) — pulverise the small leather packet rendering its contents so thin and delicate that one ounce of gold covers an area of about twelve square yards. This will later be sold to devotees to paste onto Buddha images — in the Mahamuni Pagoda in Mandalay the image has been almost surrealistically distorted by generations of gold leaf (the gold encasing alone is said to weigh several tons). Indeed the pagoda coffers are kept healthy by the collection and resale of the gold leaf droppings.

But it is the coffers of merit that provide the real motive for these curious activities. By attempting to accrue a hefty balance of this eternal currency, the pious Buddhist hopes to escape the endless "whirlpool of rebirth" and slip into Nirvana and the "calm of the first beginnings":

"If any teach Nirvana is to cease
Say unto such they lie.
If any teach Nirvana is to live
Say unto such they err."

"..... where the soil only requires to be scratched to bring forth abundant crops".

In her daily quest for Nirvana a dried fish seller donates some of her wares to a monk.

In the gentle light long
shadows merge dream and
reality; but as the fantasies of
dawn give way to the realities
of the day, the contours become
clear.

Noble Order of the Yellow Robe

"**B**UDDHISM is life to the Burman" but, until the age of twelve when the male Burmese child normally has his *Shin-pyu* ("to make a monk"), his Buddhistic life cannot commence and he is cast among the animals on the Ladder of Existence. The day he is accepted as an *upathaka* — a believer — it becomes within his power to raise or lower his status in his next life.

"Higher than Indra's eye ye may lift your lot,
Or sink it lower than the worm or gnat."

The *Shin-pyu* is an occasion of feasting. An auspicious day is chosen by the astrologer, invitations are dispensed by the female members of the family — not in the form of cards but in packets of lapet, a delicious fermented tea. As the day draws near the novice receives instruction in monastic etiquette. In some rural districts the boy is confined to his house for seven days before his initiation for fear that jealous evil spirits will kidnap him. On the due day he is dressed in princely garments and jewels, is mounted on a white pony and heads a gay procession around the village. This regal journey symbolises Prince Siddhartha's (the Gautama Buddha's) royal life, which he renounced in order to search for enlightenment. The journey ended, the boy disrobes before the head of the monastery, and has his head shaved, washed with seeds and rubbed with saffron. Then, prostrating himself before the head monk, he asks in Pali for admittance to the monastery so that he may strive towards gaining Nirvana. Once accepted he is given his robes, a begging bowl is hung around his neck and, whilst festivities continue in his house, follows the monk to his new home. Buddhism abhors physical suffering and a small boy's life in a monastery is not a hard one. He will learn and observe the ten commandments (the five most important, the Five Great Precepts, forbid taking life, stealing, adultery, lying and drinking intoxicating liquor), learn his lessons, beg for his food and carry out domestic duties in the monastery. Depending on how pious his family is his stay could be anything from one week to several months, (or indeed forever).

With a population of some 800,000 monks to house, monasteries (like pagodas) abound in Burma. So, tucked away in a secluded part of each town, village and hamlet — a monastery must not be too near noisy, secular buildings —

will be a *pongyi kyaung*. The compound is enclosed by a fence and once on the sacred ground one must remove one's shoes. In the centre of the enclosure stands the main teak or brick building, groups of well-foliaged trees casting shade over the spruce eastern courtyard and outhouses. The large trees in the compound not only provide shade and fruit, but also commemorate the Gautama Buddha's attainment of enlightenment under a banyan tree and serve as a reminder that the next Buddha is expected to receive his under a mesua ferrea. The *kyaung* is always an oblong, single-storey building — it is an indignity for anyone to be above the head of a monk — supported on pillars about eight feet from the ground: one approaches up a flight of steps onto a wooden verandah. Inside are two large rooms where the monks teach, receive devotees and chant their daily prayers. Many of these structures are ornate, decorated with magnificent carvings of dancing figures, mythical animals and patterned friezes; indeed some would have been gilded, though today they have weathered to a soft grey brown. Others, which one is apt to tumble on in the middle of the paddy, are plain and exude a simple serenity.

Monks should be up before the animal kingdom: shortly before dawn "when there is light enough to see the veins in the hand" a monastery awakes. Following meditation and prayers the monks emerge into the secular world to beg for their day's food. Eyes lowered and without any show of emotion or acknowledgement they continue until their bowls are full. Once back in the monastery the food must be consumed before midday and the rest of the day is devoted to teaching the novices, counselling and meditation.

The hierarchy of a monastery is based on length of stay. To gain the title of *pyongyi* — a great glory — a monk must have spent at least ten years in the Noble Order of the Yellow Robe. For others of the monastic community there are titles covering a wide range of circumstances: *Lu-twet* (a runaway) is a monk who has returned to the secular world; *taw-twet* (one who has fled from the jungle of the world) is the married man, who has taken the cloth; then the most revered name

Nuns hurry along the streets of Sagaing through the evening sunlight; they must reach their monastery before sundown itself.

of all *nge-byu* (white or stainless), is bestowed on those who from youth have chosen the austere monastic life. Before acceptance into the Noble Order a postulant must have reached twenty and have his parents' consent. It is said that Nanda, the Gautama Buddha's half-brother and crown prince at the time, wished to become a novice. Their father, King Thudaw-dana, was horrified at the prospect of losing two sons and extracted a promise from Buddha that parental consent would always be obtained.

A monk's material possessions are limited to the eight sacred items: three pieces of yellow cloth which make up the robe, a leather belt for securing the robe, a needle to keep it in good repair, a begging bowl, an axe for splitting firewood, and a water filter to ensure no animal life is taken. Also deemed essential is a palm fan to protect the monk from looking on females and giving rise to carnal thoughts ("women are disturbers of tranquil meditation"). But today there always seems to be a gaggle of ladies chatting and having tea in the monasteries.

Supporting Burma's substantial monastic population imposes heavy demands on the country's economy, but society expects nothing in return save the merit gained through guardianship of the monks. However, the situation was different prior to Burma's annexation by the British Empire, when the country's education was in the hands of the monks. All boys attended the monastic school free of charge where they learned about the Buddhistic scriptures and the rudiments of mathematics as well as to read and write. In those days Burma could boast the highest rate of literacy in Asia. The British started to modify this system in the nineteenth century by introducing lay and missionary schools. But it was not until after Independence that the radical changes occurred. When the Ne Win government came to power in the 1960s the Buddhist establishment was considered potential political opposition. To neutralize the support that Ne Win felt was being given to the ethnic rebels, he commanded all monks to be registered, exposed those living openly with women "under my nose" in Rangoon, and removed the education system from monastic control. Today, education is run by the state and only in the remotest areas are monastic schools to be found.

Although deprived of a practical role in society, the ubiquitous monks continue to exert a profound influence by their example (though the record, like that of all religious orders the world has ever known, is by no means unblemished), and, perhaps more important, by serving as a constant reminder of the way of Buddha. This is reflected in the reverence and piety in which they are held by the vast majority of the lay population. So far as the monks themselves are concerned their life is certainly austere, though by no means unpleasant. The calm of monastic routine, uncluttered by material paraphernalia, provides the ideal environment in which to study and adopt the teachings of the Middle Way — a life of no extremes in which every thought, word and deed should contribute towards reaching Nirvana, that "lifeless, timeless state of bliss, in which the spirit knows no joy and no sorrow, but remains perpetually contemplating the abstract truth, delivered finally from the cycle of recurring existences".

Two novice monks search for a little mischief.

A calm-faced saya-daw (head of a monastery) consults one of his tomes, ". . . a look of repose which they wear easily after years of daily meditation and freedom from petty irritations".

Home for these serious-faced novices is a beautiful carved teak monastery lost amidst the fields surrounding the once great city of Ava. Kite strings meticulously wound round the base of the building reveal the novices' favourite pastime.

As evening draws in two nuns return across the long U Bein Bridge to their monastery in Amarapoura.

Even a remote hill village will probably boast a flourishing kyaung (monastery). With the Government schools far away in the valley, parents are extra keen for their male children to have their shin-pyu (initiation ceremony) so as to enter a monastery and ensure a good education. While Buddhist boys must enter a monastery at some stage, it is not unusual to see little girls in the pale pink nun's habit.

Lords of the Great Mountain

THE beauty of a Burmese maiden is enhanced by adorning her hair with a sprig of blossom; likewise fresh flowers decorate tastefully laid out stalls in the market. These are not, as one might imagine, efforts to glamorize the "shop window" but are in fact signs of homage to the nats. Nats, or spirit gods, play an important role in the everyday life of a Burman; if not properly appeased they can prove very troublesome.

Nat worship is a legacy from before the arrival of Theravada Buddhism in Burma. Nat — meaning "lord" — was a spirit who had dominion over certain areas, objects or aspects of life. Each village had its own guardian nat who would protect all its inhabitants, as long as due deference was paid.

Both idolatry and placing one's fate in the hands of one or more gods are totally alien to the true Buddhist faith, which teaches that "no one god can help a person's salvation, it is up to the individual". Nat worship, on the other hand, is steeped in both concepts. However, by the pragmatic exercise of that most Burmese of skills — facing in two opposing directions and doing so with nonchalant ease — nat worship has been incorporated into Burmese-style Buddhism to the apparent satisfaction of all concerned. When King Anawrahta of Pagan was converted to Theravada Buddhism in late 1058, he realised that he was not going to be able to stamp out entirely the intricate web of animism, alchemy and tantric cults practised by the Ari monks and their followers. So he disbanded the elements he regarded as most irreverent, and then showed his tolerance of the nats by bringing them into the pagoda precinct. Anawrahta declared that Thagyamin, the King of the Gods and guardian of Buddhism, was to be added to the original thirty-six nats and considered their leader. Images of the thirty-seven, in attitudes of worship, were then placed in the newly-built Shwezigon Pagoda in Pagan (not to be confused with the Shwedagon in Rangoon), in order that "the people come to worship their old gods, and then they will discover the truth of the new faith of Buddhism."

Today there are still thirty-seven "inner nats" (those allowed in the pagoda), and hundreds of "outer nats". The list of thirty-seven has varied somewhat from Anawrahta's time, and is made up of a strange mélange of heroes and tragic historical characters, the majority of whom met untimely ends. The exception was Kunshaw, "The Lord of the White Umbrella" and father of Anawrahta. Kunshaw's father was killed before he was born and the throne usurped. His mother fled the court, bringing up her son in poverty. On the death of the usurper's son, Kunhsaw was proclaimed king by popular demand and, out of the goodness of his heart, took into his palace the two pregnant wives of his predecessor and made them his queens. Their sons he brought up as his own. However, on reaching adulthood, the latter persuaded their stepfather to enter a monastery and then deposed him. Years later, when Anawrahta regained the throne and offered it to his elderly father, he refused: "I am old to look upon, old in years. Be now king thyself", he protested. He died shortly afterwards and was elevated to the nathood, but as a monk not a king.

The "outer nats" shrines you will see everywhere, perched in trees or housed in little bamboo hutches along the wayside. The most evident of these are the shrines of the "house nat". On the south side of nearly every house hangs a coconut. The strips of red and yellow fabric with which these are sometimes adorned are offerings to Eing Saung, the protector of the household. In times gone by the four corner posts of the house, which were thought to be his favourite abode, were draped in white cloth.

The traditional home of the nats is Mount Popa. This lush protuberance, nearly 5,000 feet in height, sits in the middle of the arid Myingyan plain thirty miles southeast of Pagan. Popa means "flower" in Sanskrit, and Burmese legend tells that the mountain was originally the home of beautiful flower-eating ogresses who played hide-and-seek on its tangled slopes. These curious characters emerge into recorded history in the form of rebels and brigands preying on travellers on their way to Pagan. It was indeed at Mount Popa that King Anawrahta amassed his army before marching on Pagan to regain his throne.

Nats, or spirit gods, play an important role in the everyday life of a Burman; if not properly appeased they can prove very troublesome. This magnificent shrine is to be found amongst the silk weavers' guild of Amarapoura.

The chief spirit inhabitants of Mount Popa are a brother and sister, together known as Min Maha-Giri (meaning "Lords of the High Mountain") who are said to have lived around the fourth century some miles north of Pagan. Their story epitomises both the violence and essential morality inherent in nat beliefs. The brother bore the nickname "Mister Handsome" and was a "mighty blacksmith". He ate 70 pounds of rice at every meal and, when working in his forge, wielded an iron hammer of 50 viss (about 14 lb) in his right hand and one of 25 in his left. The mighty impact of the hammer against the anvil caused the earth to quake. This show of strength was too much for the neighbouring king, and he vowed to assassinate Mister Handsome, but the blacksmith was forewarned and escaped to the forest. The king then resorted to chicanery. He seduced Mister Handsome's sister, the beautiful "Golden Face", and made her his queen. "I no longer fear your brother", he assured her, "because he is now my brother also. Invite him to Tagaung and I shall make him governor of the city." In good faith, Mister Handsome accepted the king's invitation, only to be seized, tied to a saga tree and burnt alive. His betrayed sister, heartbroken, leapt onto the burning pyre and perished with her brother. On their deaths, the two were transformed into mischievous nats and took up residence in a saga tree. In revenge against their murderer, they killed all moving objects that ventured into the shade of their tree. In a state of exasperation, the king felled the tree and threw it into the Irrawaddy. When the log reached Thiripyissaya, King Thinlikyaung, who had heard the tale, pulled it from the river and on it had carved images of the brother and sister. Then with much pomp and ceremony this was transported to Mount Popa where a shrine was built and remains to this day. In A.D. 849 the Lords of the High Mountain were also appointed as the guardian nats of Pagan, and their images were carved on the pillars on either side of the city's main gates.

Nat culture remained deeply ingrained in both secular and religious matters. Included in the court oath of loyalty to the last Burmese kings (read before an image of Buddha) was the statement that by serving his royal master with obedience, the candidate "under the aid of the five thousand nats that guard religion", would be free from all ninety-six diseases. It was only with the building of Mandalay in 1857 that a particularly barbaric nat custom was brought to an end. Previously, during the construction of a new city, someone would be buried alive under each corner of the perimeter wall. These unfortunates were supposed then to be reincarnated as evil nats and to keep at bay the city's foes.

Not all nats are of such violent disposition. "The little lady of the flute" acts as guardian and playmate of children (when engaged in the latter role causing them to smile in their sleep). Happily, nat worship today manifests this gentler side of its nature, with daily offerings to one's favourite spirit to bring safety and success in one's mundane life.

At the eight cardinal points round the base of the Shwedagon Pagoda are the planetary posts. In Burmese astrology the week has eight days — the equivalent of Wednesday being split into morning and evening — with each day represented both by a planet and an animal; thus, if like these ladies, Saturday born, one takes flowers, lights a candle and pours water over the image in the "Saturday corner".

Small boats rounding a treacherous point near Akyab (in Arakan). It is necessary to drop anchor before tacking up the eastern coast.

Preparing to Greet Day

"THE Burmese are not of the mysterious East, they are of the smiling East" — an assertion amply borne out by the Burmese addiction to festivals and theatre. Like practically every important aspect of Burmese society, and in particular those involving entertainment, they take place under the auspices of the pagoda.

Burma's rainy season, during which merrymaking is impractical, coincides with the Buddhist "Lent", which marks the period of Buddha's meditation prior to his Enlightenment. They both end in October. From then until the following July every town and village will periodically buzz with a festival of some description. There are national festivals for celebrating the New Year (the Water Festival), the harvest, the end of Buddhist Lent (the Festival of Light), the presentation of new robes to the monks (the Weaving Festival) and many more. Then also each pagoda will have its own birthday festival and each community its favourite nat (spirit god) to honour. In addition special events, such as the raising of a new *hti* (umbrella) for a pagoda, will require an individual celebration.

Days before a festival, a village of bamboo stalls mushrooms around the pagoda; men, women and children dash about arranging their wares; sideshows of old-fashioned roundabouts with brightly-coloured papier-mâché animals materialize; a carefree carnival spirit permeates the air. If the festival is at one of the more renowned pagodas, pilgrims — including families with goods and chattels stuffed into bullock and pony carts — converge from far and wide.

The frenzied preparations give way to the commencement of the festival itself. As the dawn mist hovers over the festival ground the pagoda awakes. The swish of brooms can be heard as devotees sweep away the remnants of yesterday's offerings. The arrival at the flower stalls of the day's fresh produce brings a heady aroma of jasmine and rosebuds and awakens the men and women whose job it is to wire the blooms into nosegays. Fires are kindled; some prepare their own breakfast, others hunt out the *mohingha* stalls which have sprung up as if by magic. The mohingha vendor sits behind a low table covered with a multitude of bowls. These contain an eccentric-seeming variety of delicacies — chopped coriander, fried garlic, bean crackers, hard-boiled eggs, fish sausage, sesame nuts. On one side is a large basin of rice noodles, with

a muslin cloth to keep the heat in and the flies out; on the other a large cauldron of fish soup steams over a charcoal fire. Hands flickering, the vendor combines in an empty bowl, a handful of noodles, a sprinkling of each of the chopped ingredients (deftly cutting the eggs and fish sausage with scissors), a ladleful of fish broth, a pinch of chili powder and finally a squeeze of fresh lime — delicious. A popular and expert mohingha cook can serve 250 bowls single-handed at one breakfast session (about seventy an hour).

A festival may last for up to a week. During the daytime there will be bands, processions to the pagoda, dancing — an extravaganza of colour, movement and noise, especially noise — generally incorporating the particular activity which symbolizes the purpose of the festival. However, the pivot of several festivals is at night. At the end of Buddhist Lent, for example, the return of Buddha to earth is marked by lights on every conceivable building; while during the Weaving Festival, virgins compete by the light of the full moon in making new robes for the monks.

Festival evenings and nights are frequently devoted to pwès or entertainment. According to Sir George Scott, "there is no nation on the face of the earth so fond of theatrical representations as the Burmese". As light begins to fade activity centres on the large stage. The auditorium is a fenced-in area with rush matting on the ground and is free to all, so it's first come first served. The whole family settles down for the night's entertainment with bedrolls for the children and tiffin boxes. For the less provident, hawkers weave in and out selling nuts, nibbles, cigars and cigarettes. The Burmese are a nation of smokers from nearly the smallest ("Burmese children never smoke before they can walk") to the oldest grandmother who sits, intent on the pwè, an enormous cigar clenched between her gums and holding a small basin to catch the ash and sparks, for Burmese cigars behave akin to sparklers. If more substantial sustenance is required, a galaxy of food stalls with such delights as

An array of food stalls mushrooms around a festival ground, most of the delights being prepared over open fires. However some, like that of this sombre ice cream seller with his pink cones and pop art hoarding, have (by Burmese standards) "modern" equipment.

"husband and wife" onion cakes (cooked in separate moulds and then joined) is stationed around the fence. A Burmese theatre audience resembles nothing so much as a restless, constantly murmuring sea.

There are two distinct groups of pwè: light and serious drama. The first is of the variety-show genre. Burmese, like Chinese, is a monosyllabic language and affords ample opportunity for puns. However, the highly developed Burmese art of clowning with all the facial subtleties of mime, lets even the non-Burmese speaker in on most of the humour in these uproarious sketches. The second group consists of the more serious *Wethandaya Wutha* (the Ten Great Birth Stories), which illustrate the last ten incarnations of Buddha before attaining enlightenment.

Both types of theatre involve song, dance and dramatic music and the cast is supported by an orchestra eight to ten strong. The most spectacular instruments are the *saing-waing* and the *kyi-waing*; both are made of elaborately carved (and often gilded) panels standing two to three feet high and forming a circle some five feet in diameter. Suspended from the inside of the panels are either drums or gongs with the player sitting in the middle. He constantly tunes his drums by applying and kneading a sticky paste of burnt rice husk. There are no written scores so all the music must be learnt by ear. Each group has an apprentice who plays the *wa le'kot* (bamboo cymbals): the apprenticeship system ensures the music's passage from one generation to the next. This strange orchestra can produce effects ranging from the ponderous and lovelorn to the warlike and triumphant, playing for hours on end with unflagging zeal. The Western ear takes time to adjust to its discordant crashes and rhythmic eccentricities, but in time they cast a mesmeric spell. The dancers also require tremendous stamina. Of the 120 basic steps most are executed with bent knees. Lissom bodies, clad in court dress from the Ava period, perform a series of sinuous, tentacular movements. The skirt is a narrow sequined tube with the added hazard of a two-foot train which, with consummate skill and elegance, is flicked out of the way by a supple foot, without disturbing the smooth glide of the dance. The steps for men and women are the same and to see a man dancing the role of a princess is by no means unusual; in any case the Burmese male's excellent figure and sparsity of facial hair can make it difficult to tell the difference.

In early April Burmans seemingly go mad: battalions of young people line the streets armed with vats of water, from which they fill all available receptacles in order to throw the contents at hapless passersby. Only the elderly and the monks are exempt. Sir George Scott recounts the following experience of a newly arrived Englishman. "The victim reached Rangoon on the second day of the water-feast, and having no Indian outfit got himself up in a tall hat, frockcoat, and the rest . . . On the verandah he found three or four Burmese girls, who forthwith asked permission to throw water on him. He naturally supposed they were asking whether he wanted to see the master of the house, and nodded violently. Whereupon they capsized their bowls of water over him, including the hat in the libation. The astonished man took it to be a custom of the country to cool down over-heated foreigners, but thought the inclusion of his hat an unnecessary detail." This three-day orgy of water throwing marks the beginning of the New Year and the visit to earth of Thagyamin, the King of the Nats. The water is to honour the heavenly visitor, "to wash away the old year's dirtiness and to begin the new by good and auspicious deeds." The festivities start with *a-kyo nay* ("preparing to greet day"), when sacred water pots are filled and made sweet smelling by the addition of *tha-byay* leaves. Food is prepared both for the monasteries and the neighbours, and bamboo stands are erected for communal hairwashing. The noblest part of the body must be clean to honour the celestial guest. In the days of the monarchy there was a ceremonial washing *(tha-gyan daw gyi)* of the King's hair. The water for this ceremony was carried from the springs of the beautiful Gaung se kyun (Head Washing Island). This islet, near Moulmein, seemingly hangs above the water, inspiring the idea that it was suspended from the heavens by an invisible thread. The hair-washing takes place at dusk in readiness for the God's arrival at midnight. A special shampoo is used, made by soaking the dried bark of the *tha-yaw* tree, then boiling and pounding acacia seeds, then mixing the acacia powder with the tha-yaw water.

The God's arrival is heralded by a gunfire salute, the large pots are filled with water and sacred tha-byay leaves are ceremoniously emptied and so the water throwing revel begins. Children armed with water pistols ambush the unsuspecting, young maidens exchange their thin muslin blouses for ones of thicker fabric to avoid any immodesty when their garments become wet and clinging. During the next three days everyone tries to live by the Five Great Precepts (the Buddhist code of behaviour) and children are especially well-behaved. Thagyamin, they are warned, brings with him two books, one bound in dog-skin to record the names of those who are naughty, the other bound in gold for those who have gained merit. The *a-tetnay* (rising day) marks Thagyamin's return to the heavens and ends the festivities, though some enthusiastic revellers squeeze in another day declaring that he has returned to earth to collect his forgotten pipe or umbrella.

Burma's festivals have provided both origin and continuing inspiration for the development of a rich tapestry of performing arts. They fuse together fundamental ingredients of the national character — in particular religious commitment and individuality — with the Burmese gaiety and grace which I find irresistibly beguiling. Burma's long isolation has allowed her theatre, music and dance to develop almost untouched by external influences. The long-delayed advent of television raises questions about the possible violation of Burma's cultural virginity. I believe there are grounds for optimism: it is after all "in the nature of the Burmese to make festivals", and perhaps a people at once gregarious and self-sufficient will find limited appeal in the essentially solitary pursuits of electronic "home entertainment".

Along the streets of Mandalay processes an extravaganza of colour, serenaded by the discordant crashes and rhythmic eccentricities that is Burmese music. The revellers, dressed as a King, Queen and Courtiers, are raising money for a coming pagoda festival.

To celebrate the successful raising of the hti, a Karen group performs a traditional dance.

Beneath its easygoing appearance, this comic dance is a routine which requires extreme skill and vast resources of energy — hence its popularity among young male dancers.

The Motionless Flame

"IN the early mornings it gave a radiance to the clear air and the blue sky; in the daylight it shone forth like a blaze of gold, burning and pure; in the evenings it glowed softly as the breeze, tinkled its bells and filled the heart with a gentle sadness which is not grief but a sweet perception of unearthly things; and at night the lights flooded it to stand high and illumined above the dark wooded slopes of the hill." The Shwedagon Pagoda (literally "Golden Temple") shimmers above the city of Rangoon — pure beauty magically combined with an aura of legend and history.

Through the mists of tradition emerges the founding story (part of which is a remarkably close parallel to the Christian nativity story). At the end of the previous world five lotus buds sprang up on Singuttara Hill (where the pagoda stands today): from each of these plants rose a sacred bird carrying a sacred yellow robe. These robes symbolized the coming of five Buddhas who would guide the next world towards Nirvana. As foretold, four of the Buddhas have appeared in the present world. (The fifth is still awaited: his coming is expected to mark the end of this world cycle.) Each of the four has left a relic to be enshrined on Singuttara Hill; Kaukathan his staff, Gaunagon his water filter, Kathapa a piece of his robe and Gautama (the most recent Buddha) eight hairs. On the seventh day following the Enlightenment of Gautama Buddha, two Burmese merchant brothers (Taphussa and Bhalliha) were travelling with a caravan of 500 carts when, for no apparent reason, the oxen stopped "as if chained to the earth". Thereupon a nat, who had seen the merchant's mother in a previous existence, appeared, giving them the news of the Gautama Buddha's Enlightenment. The brothers arrived to pay homage to the Buddha bearing "rice cakes and honey food". In return for their allegiance the Buddha plucked eight hairs from his head and bade the brothers return to their country and enshrine them on Singuttara Hill along with the previous Buddha's relics. After an Homeric journey they arrived in Burma and enlisted the help of Sakka, the King of the Nats, to locate Singuttara Hill. Eventually, it and the relics were discovered and all the treasures enshrined together with a small pagoda atop.

Thereafter, the pagoda's history emerges from the legendary mists into half light and then recorded history. The first notable pilgrim to the Hill was King Ashoka of India, the purveyor of Theravada Buddhism and convenor of the Third Buddhist Synod. He came to pay homage to the relics in about 260 B.C. The jungle had enveloped the pagoda, and Ashoka ordered it to be cleared and restored. Successive kings continued to maintain and enlarge the pagoda, the most extensive alterations being carried out during the fifteenth century. Queen Viharadevi (or Sin Saw Bu) had the stupa raised to the height of 302 feet and, for the first time, gilded. For this she donated her weight (a slender 88 lb) in gold. The pagoda's snowball development continued as more and more accessories were added (and sometimes removed). In 1612 Felipe de Brito, the Portuguese adventurer who governed the port of Syriam for thirteen years, made off with a bronze and brass bell weighing 18,000 viss (about 2 tons) intending to recast it into a cannon. "But in the power of the Buddha" the boat bearing it to Syriam sank in the Rangoon River. (The following year Syriam was sacked by the Burmese King, and de Brito taken prisoner and impaled.)

This pagoda "of wonderful bignesse, and all gilded from the foot to the toppe" has suffered both the ravages of war and natural disasters. In 1768 six years of restoration were necessary following an earthquake which devastated the top portion: it is the result of this work that we see today. King Hsinbyushin had his craftsmen encase the exquisite lotus leaves and banana bud at the stupa's summit in solid gold — 3,538 gold and silver tiles, 10 million bricks and 100,000 brass screws were used.

Fifty years later, on 11 May 1824, British troops sailed up the Rangoon River to land unchallenged in Rangoon and immediately made the "Great Pagoda" their key position. "Considered as military post" said T.A. Trant, a British staff officer, "the Dagon was of utmost importance, its elevated brick terraces, which obviated the necessity of additional fortifications, and its commanding situation rendering it the key of our whole position". This occupation was shortlived, but a little less than thirty years later the foreign military

". . . . . a beautiful winking wonder that blazed in the sun".

presence returned. In April 1852, a flotilla of fifteen warships and fifteen steamers (under the command of Rear Admiral Charles Austen, brother of the novelist Jane Austen) sailed into Rangoon carrying 6,000 men and thirty-five pieces of artillery. This time the British troops had to fight to gain control of the strategic pagoda; having driven out the Burmese, they remained in occupation for 77 years until 1929. Shamefully, the temptations of their surroundings proved impossible to resist: "there is a soldier busy with his pickaxe", observed W.F.B. Laurie, historian of the Second Burmese War, "excavating a huge golden image with as much coolness as if he were digging a trench. He is looking for treasure." One officer ordered a passage 100 feet long to be dug into the bowels of the Shwedagon stupa; he claimed, under questioning, that the purpose was to ascertain whether it could be used as a gunpowder magazine. Perhaps the most serious act of British vandalism against the Great Pagoda was the attempted removal of the vast Singu Min bell; however, this project met a similar fate to that of de Brito two and a half centuries earlier. The raft on which it was being transported to a waiting ship capsized and the attempt was abandoned. Later the people of Rangoon salvaged the bell and reinstated it in the pagoda.

The Shwedagon is "calm and sublime, with the smiling look as is seen on the face of Buddha, not smiling in the eyes or mouth but in the serene expression of inward calm". Considering the Great Pagoda's haphazard evolution, this totality of impact on the spirit as well as on the eye is all the more remarkable. We know that the original was of modest dimensions and that it has been cased and recased at least seven times. Yet surely the fluent line of the stupa's main curve and the perfect proportions in relation to its mouldings and lotus petals reflect a single conception.

The Shwedagon's secrets are only gradually vouchsafed. Beckoned by a distant vision of the "golden spire shining like a motionless flame" the pilgrim must climb Singuttara Hill via one of the four long enclosed stairways. The eyes become accustomed to the sudden darkness, the nose to the heady scent of *thanaka*, jasmine and sandalwood, and he finds himself in an Aladdin's cave of "Nirvana goods" — stalls with fantastical headdresses, Buddha images, religious tomes, gold leaf, monks' paraphernalia, lacquerware, thanaka wood cosmetics and, near the top, layer upon layer of fragrant blooms waiting to be bought as offerings. On reaching the stairway's head he is faced not with the stupa but a glittering Shrine Hall. He turns to the left — a pilgrim must go left about keeping the pagoda to the right — and the secret is revealed. First the golden mass of the lower stupa's bell shape (Buddha's inverted begging bowl) imposes itself upon his attention; then his eyes are drawn upwards to the banana bud, past the delicate tracery of the *hti* (see Glossary), its myriad jewels twinkling in the sun and bells gently stirring in the breeze and then out into the infinite beyond.

As our pilgrim's spirit returns to earth he finds all around him the calm activity of a religious village. For a great pagoda is the focus of secular as well as religious life and none more than the Shwedagon. Businessmen come to worship and then settle down to negotiate a deal, students to read, families to picnic — all gaining inspiration and strength from the environment. Many visit the pagoda to pay respects to their planetary post. In Burmese astrology the week has eight days — Wednesdays being split into morning and evening — with each day represented both by a planet and an animal. "The planet of a man's birthday will be the main guardian of his fate but at each particular period of a man's life a particular planet throws upon him its baneful or its beneficial influence". *The thin-bon-gyi* (the great basket of learning, in other words the Burmese alphabet) is divided between the eight days of the week, and it used to be customary to incorporate into a person's name the letters corresponding to his birthday. At the eight cardinal points round the base of the pagoda are the planetary posts: thus if born on a Sunday, one takes flowers, lights a candle and pours water over the image in the "Sunday corner".

Dawn or dusk are the Great Pagoda's best times. The glow of the setting sun catches the golden spire, softening its timeless lines. Pilgrims, lost in their world of prayer and acts of devotion, are engulfed in a dream-like haze. Wandering the marble terraces, warm to the feet following the day's fierce sun and marvelling at the splendour all around, Ralph Fitch, a sixteenth-century merchant adventurer, came to a simple conclusion: "it is the fairest place, as I suppose, that is in the world."

The Shwedagon awakes, the newly risen sun catching its gold and mosaic. The air is heady with morning magic and the scent of flowers. The only noise is the constant murmur from far above of the bells of the hti "moved by the wind to give sweet testimony to all spirits, and give the praying devotee a tinkling reassurance of his merit".

. . . . . pure beauty magically combined with an aura of legend and history.

53

Top right *It is thought very important to pay respects to one's planetary post; "the planet of a man's birthday will be the main guardian of his fate". Bottom Behind this devotee lost in prayer sits the Wa-thom-da-ray, the Guardian Angel of the Earth. When the world was engulfed by a Great Fire it is said she first soaked her long tresses of hair (which can be seen winding round her body) and then wrung them out to extinguish the blaze. Above Nuns must shave their heads to remove the temptation of beautification. These lay, holy women who live within the Shwedagon Pagoda precinct and perform the domestic chores of the pagoda, follow suit.*

Opposite *In 1782 King Bodawpaya's astrologers recommended the transfer of his capital from Ava to Amarapoura, where many of the secular buildings, including the U Bein Bridge, were dismantled and reconstructed.*

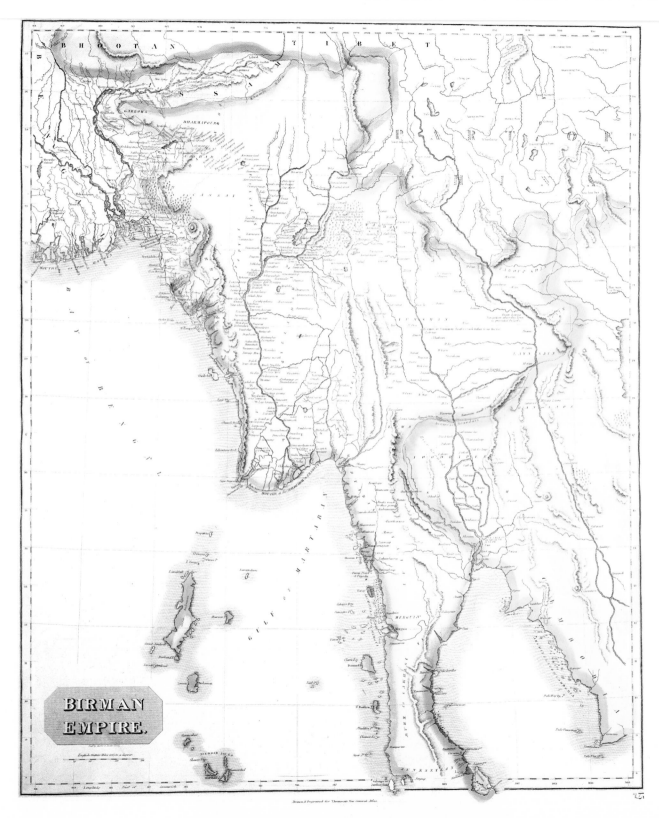

BIRMAN EMPIRE.

Nineteenth-Century Map of Burma

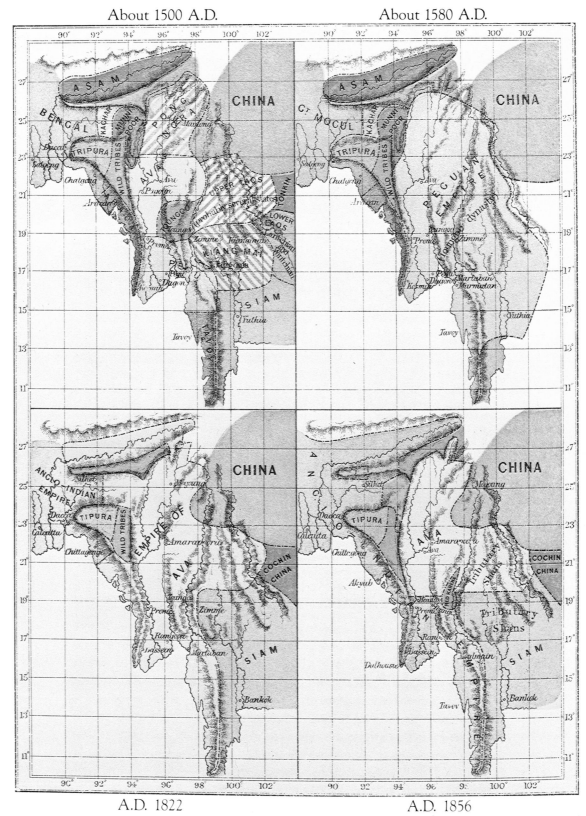

About 1500 A.D.

About 1580 A.D.

A.D. 1822

A.D. 1856

Historical Geography of the Burmese Countries at Several Epochs

River of Lost Footsteps

T HE Irrawaddy, "huge and ochreous", is the lifeline of Burma. From its source in the eastern Himalayas the great river sweeps down from the heart of Asia to the Indian Ocean. "So immense is the volume of water that pours down the Irrawaddy, even in the low-water season, that the suspended silt is carried far out to sea and long before an incoming ship is within sight of land, the sea turns from clear blue to milky green and finally to thick, browny yellow." For centuries, the river was the main trade route from the Indian Ocean upstream into China, as it were through the back door. Navigable for 1,000 miles, it provided polity, prosperity and mobility to the Burmese, but also, and less welcome, access for foreign invaders to the very heart of the kingdom.

The waters of this noble kingdom bustle with an assortment of curious craft: perhaps none so eccentric as the *hnau* with its ladder-like mast from which was suspended a curved 65-foot yard arm, carrying a 130-foot sail. "These boats can scarcely sail, of course, except before the wind", observed Sir Henry Yule in 1855. "A fleet of them speeding before the wind has a splendid though fantastic appearance. With their vast spreading wings and almost invisible hulls, they look like a flight of colossal butterflies skimming the water." Today, alas, the hnau are no longer, but they have spawned many interesting progeny. The ferries which journey the 1,000 miles from Bhamo in the north down to the delta, although now diesel-powered, are essentially the same as the royal steamers and those used by that quintessential by-product of the British Empire, the Irrawaddy Flotilla Company. They hardly present a very nautical bearing: their two passenger decks are more aptly described as "floors", and definitely they have windows rather than portholes. Their outward appearance is somewhat shabby but this again seems consistent with their pedigree. "The royal steamers were driven until their machinery broke down", and were then "allowed to strand themselves and blister and rot away in the sun".

A trip on one of these delightful craft certainly provides the best vantage point from which to observe the "kingly stream" and the society it supports. The vessel slowly slaloms between the sandbanks — a man in the bow occasionally bringing out a bamboo pole to test the depth. With a self-important hoot to announce her arrival she heads for a group of people patiently waiting onshore and sedately glides onto the mud bank. Gangplanks are extended at a steep angle: though soon muddied and slippery, they are negotiated nimbly by those embarking and disembarking, wide baskets balanced on their heads, and often further laden with a child or two.

With the advent of the monsoon, however, riverine life acquires an urgent quality: now "its sluggish stream swells over the summit of its banks". No longer do the small skiffs — piled high with earthenware pots or the haphazardly strung together rafts of teak logs, skipper's hut perched atop — meander downstream but race along. "Whole villages were passed with the water spreading beneath the houses, and with their carts hung up to the trees to prevent their being floated off by the current", recounts Sir Henry Yule, who found himself on the river in such circumstances. Each craft carries an offering to its guardian nat, and along the bank are shrines to appease nats who otherwise might "vex the boatmen" during difficult navigation.

The Irrawaddy has played a central role in Burmese history, for the past 600 years or so, perhaps *the* central role. For control of the river meant control of the vital north-south communications, control of the economy and control of the backdoor into China. Kipling bestowed on the Irrawaddy the melancholy title "River of the Lost Footsteps", referring particularly to the tragic Anglo-Burmese wars of the nineteenth century; but the river has provided a theatre for so many wars that the name must be considered as apt as "Elephant of India" with its pacific connotations of great size and stately, measured pace. In fact, the origin of the name Irrawaddy comes from Sanskrit *Iravati*, meaing "River of Refreshment". The ubiquitous Yule captures both the poetic and menacing aspects of the river thus: "the great elbow of the river below us, mirroring the shadows of the woods on its banks, and the glowing clouds above, had been like a lake,

"Cloud Vessel" sedately slides onto a mud bank at one of her numerous ports of call on the Irrawaddy. The river is navigable from Bassein on the coast to Bhamo 1,000 miles to the north.

were it not for the downward drift of the war-boats."

It was not in fact until the fourteenth century that the most strategic area, halfway up the Irrawaddy's navigable waters (around present-day Mandalay) was settled. Thence it was possible both to control the river highway and to guard the "smiling fields of rice" from Chinese and Shan invaders. Accordingly, for the next 500 years until the annexation of Upper Burma by the British in 1886, the capital oscillated between Sagaing, Ava, Amarapoura and finally Mandalay.

"Cities have risen, their palaces and pagodas reflected in the swift running waters, and then vanished", reclaimed by the ever encroaching jungle. The successful monarch was not only expected to have military and economic control of the river, he was also relied upon to exercise dominion over its physical behaviour. When in the late eighteenth century the flood waters were reaching a dangerous level, King Bodawpaya was advised by his ministers that a royal command was required to abate them. On an auspicious day a stately pageant was staged during which the King ordered the river to subside. Thanks no doubt to his ministers' meteorological knowledge, it duly did.

The early fifteenth century saw the advent of European traders, some of whom penetrated far up the Irrawaddy, lured by the fables of Ava, "in which grow rubies and many other precious stones". One such was Nicole de Conti, the first Westerner to give an eye-witness account of Burma. He sailed up the river to Ava which, he reported, was "a city more noble than all the others, the circumference of which is fifteen miles". However, for the next 300 years the Europeans, having opened up more abundant mercantile hunting grounds, were content merely to flirt with Burma. Thus she remained on the sidelines of the main trade routes from the Arabian Gulf to Southern India through the Malacca Straits to China.

Ironically it was King Alaungpaya, the founder of Burma's last dynasty who, in the course of leading his country onto one of those rare "white squares of 'internationalism'" at the start of the eighteenth century, rekindled European interest in Burma. His capture of Manipur and parts of Assam stimulated the East India Company to despatch one Captain Baker to negotiate a treaty. He arrived at Ava bearing gifts of gunpowder and muskets. Far from greeting him with the expected enthusiasm Alaungpaya rejected him outright: "Have I asked or do I want any assistance to reduce my enemies to subjection? Let none conceive such an opinion!" Crestfallen and with no treaty fixed, the captain returned south to the East India Company's base at Cape Negrais, but found the Irrawaddy as confusing to navigate as were Burmese politics. "The width of the apparent river was excessive, and it was difficult to guess where the proper channel lay."

It was not for another century that Britain made any progress in relations with Burma and then only by dint of gunboat diplomacy, and as ever the conduit was the Irrawaddy. King Bodawpaya, in the process of enlarging his kingdom, had captured Arakan and thus had given Burma a common border with British India. His successor continued with this expansionist policy with frequent raids into Assam and Chittagong until in 1824 the British were provoked into declaring war. A difficult disease-ridden campaign followed with British troops advancing up the Irrawaddy as far as Prome. But King Bagyidaw dismissed the massive territorial concessions that were extracted from him in the subsequent treaty of Yandabo with superb nonchalance. (The British were enraged by what they considered his arrogance in the "most grandiose fashion".) "The white strangers from the west", Bagyidaw announced, "fastened a quarrel upon the Lord of the Golden Palace. They landed at Rangoon, took that place and Prome; and were permitted to advance as far as Yandabo, for the King, from motives of piety and regard to life, made no effort whatever to oppose them." However, there could be no doubt that their use of the Irrawaddy enabled the East India Company to gain a decisive victory. Just thirty years later the two adversaries were once again locked in conflict. The outcome was the same, only this time the whole of Lower Burma was annexed by the British.

It was fear for control of the Irrawaddy which caused a third Anglo-Burmese war in 1885. Growing French influence in the north of Burma was a source of agitation to the British in the south: but they were ignorant of a comprehensive treaty, including crucial shipping rights on the river, that the French were secretly negotiating with King Theebaw. In the finest Gallic tradition it was an affair of the heart which actually sparked off the war. Fanny Moroni, a Eurasian favourite at court in Mandalay and lady-in-waiting to Queen Supyalat, was also the mistress (and of course confidante) of the deputy French Consul, one Monsieur Bonvilleu. Her lover compounded his indiscretions by returning to Mandalay from a spell of home leave with a French wife. In revenge, the horrified Fanny divulged the details of the French secret plans to the British. The subsequent war consisted of a straightforward push up the Irrawaddy to Mandalay and lasted but a few months, with scant resistance from the Burmese army. Sir George Scott's portrait, though rather unkind, is somewhat consistent with the circumstances of tragic reality that we know existed with Theebaw's court: "the soldiers were very gorgeous. Peony, roses and sunflowers were as nothing to them. . . The helmets do not suit at all with long hair. The top knot of a good many is so large that the pickelhouse balances on it and wobbles about in a most undignified fashion."

With King Theebaw deported to Calcutta and the whole of Burma now under British control, the Irrawaddy soon became a hive of commercial activity, with the Irrawaddy Flotilla Company vessels carrying some nine million passengers a year (some in luxury paddlesteamers complete with polished brass fittings). The Company advertised that their freight included "silk, tamarind, marble Buddhas, elephants sometimes". Burma's riches were now sucked into British colonial trade — teak logs lashed together and floated down river; rice from the Irrawaddy's fertile plains ("where the rice grew of itself") and lastly crude oil.

At Yenangyaung (meaning "fetid-water rivulet"), on the east bank of the Irrawaddy, oil literally bubbled to the surface. ("The town proclaims the nature of its staple to nose and eyes.") It seems that the Burmese have used this readily available resource since the thirteenth century in their lamps, as a wood preservative and even consumed it as a medicine. By 1855 the demand for oil had increased — it was used, for example, in the manufacture of candles in England — so the wells had to be dug deeper.

"Frequently the diggers became senseless from the exhalations", reported Yule. According to one of his informants, "if a man is brought to the surface with his tongue hanging out, it is a hopeless case. If his tongue is not hanging out, he can be brought round by hand-rubbing and kneading his body all over". The wells were the private property of twenty-three families who intermarried to preserve their monopoly. In Henry Yule's time their *Myo-Thoo-gyee* (mayor or leading spokesman) was also the *Myit-Tsim-woon* (Chief Magistrate of the river).

Notwithstanding all the turbulence and tragedy to which it has borne witness, serene and unmoved as the image of Buddha, the great river flows on — gliding past the "cockpit of Kingship" at Ava, the pagodas of Pagan, the barren heights of Yenangyaung, and the "smiling paddy fields" to its delta and finally out into the Indian Ocean. The Irrawaddy's strategic importance has declined considerably, the railways, roads and even aeroplanes of today's Burma having broken the river's monopoly of communications; and presumably external threats to the country can be considered, at worst, minor. However, as a source of irrigation for its spreading plains and thereby of food for much of Burma, it remains an irreplaceable asset. Also for most of its riverside communities the Irrawaddy serves as the primary source of water, and its bank provide the site for numerous household tasks, in particular the daily washing ritual. Evening is the time for collecting water. Oxen drawing elegant carts process across the sand banks and wade out into the stream, where their masters ladle water into their barrels. Watching this scene against the sunset at Pagan — the many-spoked wheels creaking under their loads against a background of villagers' chatter and the occasional cry from out on the river — is to witness part of Burma's essence: a people in contented harmony with their environment, timeless in a settled land.

Each evening as dusk falls a domestic scene unfurls on the shore of the Irrawaddy River. *"There is in Burmese life a beauty that delights the eye and a dignity that makes one feel proud of the human race"*.

63

*Evening is the time for
collecting water. Oxen drawing
elegant carts process across the
sand banks and wade out into
the stream, where their masters
ladle their barrels full.*

Looking across the Irrawaddy from the "pagoda sprinkled heights of Sagaing" to where once stood that "cockpit of kingship", Ava. "The sight, with the background of the huge dark Shan Hills to the eastward, is striking and beautiful in the extreme", wrote Sir George Scott in 1886.

Lords of the White Elephant

THE capitals of Burma have been peripatetic for centuries. It was not until 1044 — and then only for relatively short periods of time — that Burma was unified, having previously been a collection of warring states. "The political kaleidoscope was ever turning round, the countries were still there, but several sovereignties were jumbled together in new forms." To read a straight history of the whys and wherefores is frankly dizzy-making. Rather, I have attempted to sketch in outline some of the main elements of this tortuous tale, colouring in occasional sections of the canvas with glimpses of contemporary life in some of Burma's many capital cities as seen through the eyes of travellers from the West. These include men of God, mammon or empire — sixteenth-century merchants such as Caesar Frederick the Venetian; Father Manrique, the Portuguese Jesuit who lived at the court of King Thiri-thu-dhamma in the 1630s; and Ralph Fitch, chartered by Elizabeth I of England; as well as three observant and highly literate colonials, Sir Henry Yule and Sir George Scott representing the nineteenth century, and Maurice Collis the twentieth.

From about the third century B.C. there were three main areas of civilisation. To the west in what is now Arakan, there ruled a dynasty at Wethali (there is a "formal list" of the Kings of Arakan from 2666 B.C.–A.D. 1784); in the east was the first Mon Empire whose capital was Thaton (between where Pegu and Moulmein are today); and then on the Irrawaddy the Pyu settlement at Sri Ksetra (now Prome). However, as Father Sangermano warns us, "even on the origin and progress of the Burmese monarchy, the reader must be prepared to meet nothing in their annals but marvellous tales, mixed up with very little truth." There remains little readily visible of these cities today but the occasional city wall and pagoda. At Wethali (Vesali), however, an archaeological dig has been in progress since 1979: so far a red brick fort 85 feet by 60 feet has been unearthed, its outer wall 8 feet thick and 15 feet high and surrounded by a moat. In peacetime this fort was used as an assembly hall. Next to it is the palace, unexcavated at the time of writing. (This may pose a problem as it is now the site of a village.)

Pagan, on the east bank of the Irrawaddy and virtually at the centre of the country, took the centre of the stage also when in 1044 King Anawrahta seized the throne. By 1056 he had unified the country, irrigated the rice fields and most important of all, been converted to Theravada Buddhism. This was the start of one of Burma's short excursions into internationalism. Pagan, with its proud army of pagodas, became the world capital of Theravada Buddhism. Anawrahta conceived the idea of a Buddhistic Empire to challenge the doctrinal dominance of the Indians and Chinese. "The Burmese people", observes the Burmese historian, Dr. Htin Aung, "began to consider themselves as champions of the Indo-Chinese peninsula, whose peoples were tied to them by the silken threads of Buddhism." Not until 1287, when allegedly "1,000 large arched temples, 1,000 smaller ones, and 4,000 square temples" were destroyed in an unsuccessful attempt to fortify the city against the advancing army of Kublai Khan, did Pagan lose its living glory. Today Pagan's remains, scattered across a vast arid plain, positively exude that elusive "pleasure of ruins" quality. From the terrace of Thatbinnyu — Pagan's tallest pagoda — the Irrawaddy forms a great elbow on two sides with a strange spur of hills to the east, and into the hazy distance the plain erupts with pagodas, of all shapes, sizes and degrees of decay. The jingle of a pony trap disturbs the quiet to remind one that Pagan and the adjoining village of Nyaung-oo still harbour life.

Owing to its aridity — possibly a result of the drastic deforestation required to feed the pagoda builders' hungry brick kilns — the plain supports little agriculture. The local community must rely instead on fishing, weaving and lacquerware production, as well as of course the income from visitors. Pagan has been producing fine lacquerware since the time of King Anawrahta. It is not quite clear whether the King imported the craft from Nanchao (modern-day Yunnan Province of China) — which he visited in an attempt to acquire Buddha's tooth — or whether it was brought by the artisans from the conquered Mons, whom he resettled in Pagan. The majority of these lacquer articles are for domestic

The beautiful Ananda Pagoda, whose site was foretold by the Gautama Buddha, rises in graduated terraces to a height of 168 feet.

use, such as betelboxes, *bi-it* ladies' toilet boxes and drinking cups. "The supreme test of excellence is when the sides will bend in till they touch without cracking."

Of the "four great pagodas" of Pagan, to which local folklore attributes various superlative qualities, Gawdawpalin (the most elegant), Ananda (the most beautiful), Dhamayangyi (the most massive) and Thatbyinnyu (the highest), Ananda, built in 1091, holds the most fascination. Whitewashed so it stands apart from the rest and shaped like a perfect Greek cross, it rises in graduated terraces to a height of some 170 feet. One enters along a "wooden colonnade, covered with carved gables and tapering slender spires" at the far end of which a shaft of light falls on the face and shoulders of a beautiful gold Buddha. This image, 31 feet tall, stands on a carved lotus pedestal. Around the central core of the pagoda pose three other statuesque Buddhas of similar size encircled by "two concentric and lofty corridors". Lining these corridors are hundreds of tiny images housed in niches. The four vast images represent the four Buddhas of the present world. Some suggest that Gautama, the most recent Buddha, was placed on the western side to give him a view across the Irrawaddy to the Tan-kye Hill and Pagoda, "where Gautama himself stood with his favourite disciple, Ananda, and predicted the future building and greatness of the City of Pagan".

Following the fall of Pagan in 1287, Burma once again declined into a "series of petty kingdoms, busy with their own petty affairs, and well protected from the outside world in their little shell". But from this concoction of states emerges some fascinating power play. The Mon capital was moved in 1365 from Martaban on the east coast to Pegu (in those days a seaside port), giving the Mons control of Lower Burma; to the north a Shan Kingdom was dominant and in the west the Arakanese moved their capital in 1433 to Mrauk-U (Myohaung).

The ensuing events are hard to credit without an appreciation of the Burmese Buddhist concept of the Universal Sovereign. "The great wheel-turning King, the holy and Universal Sovereign, a character who appears once in a cycle, at the period when the waxing and waning term of human life has reached its maximum of an *asankya* in duration" is how Yule expresses the idea, according to Maurice Collis. The Universal Sovereign "would appear as a Buddhist figure of the highest conceivable rank, maybe it would turn out that he was Maitreya, the Saviour long foretold". To achieve the status of Universal Sovereignty the monarch must be in possession of the Seven Gems (precious things). This is where Hindu and Buddhist traditions become intermingled as the Buddha denied worldly possessions. The seventh of these Gems was a White Elephant. "Every Burmese king", attests Sir George Scott, "longed for the capture of such a treasure during his reign as a token that his legitimate royalty is recognised by the unseen powers". This was perhaps because the Gautama Buddha's final incarnation before attaining Nirvana was a White Elephant. As a result, the Lord White Elephant seems to have played a seminal role in the wars that plagued Burma during the next several hundred years.

From 1550 to 1564 King Bayin-naung, based in Pegu, was consolidating his power and wealth, which in turn was attracting "merchant strangers", and "merchants of the Countrie, for there are the greatest doings and the greatest trade". Caesar Frederick, a Venetian, visited the great city in 1563 and reported that Bayin-naung involved himself extensively in affairs of trade and in consequence :"the King doeth take it for a most great affront to bee deceived of his Custome; . . . but rubies, saphrys and spinals pay no custome in nor out, because they are found growing in that country". By 1564 this powerful monarch had conquered the Shan Kingdom to the north and Chiangmai to the east. His most devastating victory was at Ayutthia, then the capital of Siam.

The Portuguese monk, Faria y Sousa, reported his triumphant return to Pegu thus: "He came at last in a chariot with the conquered queens laden with jewels at his feet, and drawn by the captive princes and lords"; following no doubt the four white elephants which were his most treasured prize. Five years later the English merchant, Ralph Fitch, visited Pegu and was allowed to view — for the payment of one ducat — the single surviving white elephant. "When he is washed and cometh out of the river, there is a gentlemen which doth wash his feet in a silver basin".

In 1599, King Razagyri of Arakan noted the waning power

The sixteen square miles of Pagan are "thickly studded with pagodas of all shapes and sizes". Great monuments stand alongside small chaotic neighbours with grass "hairdos".

of the Mon Kingdom, seized his opportunity and sacked Pegu. He carried away not only his rival king's daughter and the treasures from Ayutthia, but also the same surviving white elephant, "which in his eyes", asserts Father Manrique, "was of greater value than all the kingdoms of the world". This prize enabled him to authenticate his regime by using the title "Lord of the White elephant" (Hsin Hpyu Shin) which he had inscribed on his coins.

Arakan and its capital, Mrauk-U, or Myohaung as it is called today, now began a golden era. Up the coast at Dianga there was a sizeable Portuguese community which had been a legitimate trading post. However, its inhabitants had degenerated into pirates and slavers: they were kidnapping approximately 3,400 people annually and forcing 2,000 of them to be baptised. Razagyri turned this nuisance to advantage by enlisting them to guard his northwest frontier. The King also kept a fifty-strong Portuguese bodyguard, one of whom, Felipe de Brito, was in 1600 appointed Governor of Syriam, the southern outpost of the Arakan Kingdom. To reach Myohaung then (as today) it was necessary to take a long boat trip through a maze of creeks as the city itself is on the water. The houses stood on wooden posts, the roofs thatched with palm leaves and the walls made of bamboo matting, but "the princes and grandees", continues Father Manrique, "have wooden walls to their palaces which are ornamented with carvings and gilt mouldings".

Singuttara Hills, half a day's journey to the north of Mrauk-U, was the site of Arakan's most fabled possession, the Mahamuni Image. This statue of Buddha (several tons of metal and gold) was made by a "heavenly sculptor" during a visit of the Gautama Buddha to Singuttara Hill, and is said to be one of the five contemporary images. (Of the rest, legend has it that two are in India and two in paradise!) Father Manrique describes the pomp and circumstance involved in a royal pilgrimage to the Hill: the King himself travelling on a raft which was a replica of his Mrauk-U palace, and how he and his court "shimmered and glowed as they surged up the slope". Arakan's other treasures were also shown to Father Manrique. He was led through chambers "panelled with scented timbers such as sandalwood and eaglewood". Arriving at the "House of Gold" (the walls of which were indeed plated with gold and along the ceiling crept a gold vine), he exclaimed, "I have seen very many rich and valuable things in other parts of the east but when they opened the casket for me and I saw the *Chauk-na-gat* (earrings) I was thunderstruck". The Father was also presented to the King's ultimate pride and joy, the Lord White Elephant. "I can say that when he went out, even on an ordinary occasion, as in springtime to take his bath, he was conducted there under a white canopy embroidered with the insignia of royalty, and to the sound of music. Following him were servants with golden water-heaters, ewers, scrapers, and other golden utensils of the bath."

In 1784, the Burmese King Bodawpaya invaded Arakan, succeeded in recovering all the prizes taken by the Arakanese almost two centuries before and, in addition, carried away the Mahamuni Image. Throughout the centuries this image had symbolized Arakan's strength and autonomy. "It was their head, their life blood, their very soul", and with its disappearance so vanished their kingdom.

Myohaung today is no longer the brilliant bustling metropolis of Father Manrique's day, but retains a faded beauty. To approach the city, the ancient river steamer turns from the wide Kaladan River and picks its way up a small creek, manoeuvering between many small craft and the huge trees that dip in the water. Green hills crowned with pagodas dominate the middle distance. Having disembarked one walks along the road — no waterways now but also, other than the two boasted by the Town Council, no cars. The streets are still lined with bamboo and mat houses, but of the palace only sections of the wall remain. Nearby some of the imposing pagodas still stand, in good condition. The Shittaung Pagoda, a huge grey wedding cake and strangely un-Burmese, contains the Coronation Hall and King's Meditation Room (which was used by the Japanese to store ammunition during the war). Numerous grassy protuberances punctuate the surrounding plain — pagodas awaiting restoration, according to the Archaeology Department.

Following the loss of the Mahamuni Image, the scene moved back to the Irrawaddy; to Ava, Amarapoura, Sagaing and finally in 1857 to Mandalay. The secular buildings in these cities were constructed of wood and have either succumbed to the passage of time or were dismantled when the capital in question was moved, leaving only the pagodas to bear witness to this period of Burmese history. One wooden palace, now the Shwe Nandaw Monastery, has in fact survived in Mandalay. King Mindon died there and his son, feeling it to be an inauspicious building, had it removed from the Palace compound, and fortuitously preserved it for posterity. The compound was razed to the ground by British bombs in 1945.

Sagaing was the earliest (1315) of the capitals in this "cockpit of kingship". Its hills positively sparkle with pagodas, built "on every practicable spot of the ascent": today its 600 monasteries house some 5,000 monks and nuns. Across the water lies Ava, which was capital for some 500 years up to 1783 (then briefly again from 1823 and 1841). Few if any foreigners seem to have visited Ava and reported what they found during that period. Sir Henry Yule was of course sent on his Mission to the Court at Ava in 1855 but by then (though the Kingdom continued to be named Ava) the actual capital had been moved upstream to Amarapoura. He leaves this brief picture of the city by then in decay. "Its walls split by banyans and tufted with other growth, and behind them in the reflected glow stood up the pinnacles of bat-infested shrines." Today a sleepy existence is maintained by Ava's inhabitants, their main industry being a lacquerware factory which specializes in monks' begging bowls.

In the City of Immortals, Amarapoura, built in 1782 by Arakan's vanquisher, King Bodawpaya, the clack-clack from the looms of the cotton and silk weavers has replaced the bustle of its erstwhile 200,000 inhabitants (now reduced to one or two thousand at most). Meanwhile, in a grove of majestic trees nearby, forgotten pagodas crumble. From his new city to the pagoda where he had installed the revered Mahamuni Image, King Bodawpaya constructed "an elaborate raised causeway, paved and parapetted through with brickwork". So auspicious a place was it deemed to be that the route was lined with monasteries, "undoubtedly the most magnificent in the whole country".

Upstream, King Mindon, Burma's penultimate king, built Mandalay, the last of Burma's royal capitals, and transferred the court there in 1857. Mindon's motives in building Mandalay were both religious and secular. There was an ancient prophecy that to mark the 2,400th anniversary of the Gautama Buddha's birth a religious centre would be built on this site: and King Mindon was a deeply religious man. He was also a saddened man. By then the British had occupied half his country (the half which contained the greatest religious monument of all, the Shwedagon Pagoda, which he was never allowed to visit). He was constantly reminded of the British presence by the hoots from the Irrawaddy Flotilla Company's vessels as they plied up and down the river. And so to fulfil the prophecy and as a gesture to the British of his continued potency as a monarch, he created the City of Gems. Sir George Scott sets the scene; "on the plain between the wide sweep of the Irrawaddy and the sheer forest-clad heights of the Shan hills stood the city, its rose-red walls mirrored in the quiet lotus-strewn water of the moat . . . yellow robed monks and ragged soldiers, laughing market girls with flowers in their hair and baggy-trousered tribesmen from beyond the mist blue hills were all to be encountered on those busy sunlit thoroughfares". The splendid palace buildings of lacquered teak, many decorated with mosaics, were set amid formal gardens. To a Westerner, there was however an eyesore — the corrugated iron roofs "the invention of which must rank among the major crimes of the western world". But to Mindon they were both practical and almost the ideal colour (traditionally a king was supposed to live beneath silver roofs) and they were also reminiscent of the Great Khan's fabled palaces of shining roofs. Sir George Scott complained of the city transport, the Mandalay bullock-cart "gay enough to look at", but "the unlucky passenger very shortly discovered that there were bones in parts of his body where previously he had imagined all was soft". In further celebration of Buddha's anniversary, Mindon built the Kuthodaw Pagoda and convened the Fifth Buddhist Synod. He surrounded the pagoda with 729 tiny *pitaka* pagodas, each one containing a marble tablet inscribed in Pali with a passage from the Tripitika. (This same exercise is at the time of writing being carried out in Rangoon by ex-President U Nu, convenor of the Sixth Buddhist Synod, but this time translated into the Burmese language.) Of course supplementing still further Mandalay's importance as a religious centre was possession of the same

With the clear light of day the myriad pagodas lose their ethereal quality. Instead they are a testament to the city's former greatness, when Pagan was the world capital of Theravada Buddhism. At that time, observes Dr. Htin Aung, "the Burmese people began to consider themselves as champions of the Indo-Chinese peninsula, whose people were tied to them by the silken threads of Buddhism".

Mahamuni Image, captured by King Bodawpaya three quarters of a century before. Last but by no means least of Mindon's treasures was his White Elephant, by all accounts a surly fellow. On one occasion his "Lordship" trampled a man to death. Worried that the incident would harm the elephant's merit, the King inquired what had happened. The official in charge of the elephant's entourage, who held ministerial rank, assured Mindon: "pray do not be disturbed; it was not a man, only a foreigner."

Today Mandalay is a thriving city, looking much as Mindon left it — except that within the moat and four square ramparts (a mile for each side) of his palace, all that survives is a model of the exotic fantasy. Scrub jungle, and a military base complete with a (grounded) British Spitfire have replaced the pleasure gardens in which the Burmese court frolicked and schemed away its final years. The city acts as a market place for goods from the north (both legitimate and smuggled) as well as being, in Burmese terms, a substantial industrial centre. Its large artistic community is divided into guilds, each concerned with a different manufacturing craft: bronze casting, gold and silver ware, marble Buddha sculpting, woodcarving and the like — no whirring machinery, just time-honoured skills learnt during years of apprenticeship practised on the ground under the craftsman's house or on the sun-baked earth around it.

In the heart of Rangoon stands the Sule Pagoda. Here is one of Burma's strange contradictions: this statement of Buddhist calm acts as a traffic island at one of the city's few busy intersections.

Top right *This fine clock is one of the many relics from Queen Victoria's Jubilee (1887) still to be found in Burma.* Top left *Excavation of a fort in progress at Wethali (Vaseli).* Bottom right *The moat and castellated walls of the fabled "Golden City" of Mandalay. A mere 140 years ago royal barges "gilt from stem to stern" glided among the lotus blossom while, behind the palace walls, the most heinous crimes were perpetrated.* Above Mist *hovers over an early morning market scene. A pyramid of glossy tomatoes and a round of green chilies with young aubergines as a centrepiece, tempt prospective buyers.*

The Golden Land

"NOW, if bountiful Providence had put you in a pleasant damp country where rice grew of itself and fish came up to be caught, putrified and pickled, would you work?" Indeed, Burma chroniclers down the ages have noted the Burmese propensity for enjoying what we might nowadays call a relaxed lifestyle. "If two-thirds of your girls were grinning, good humoured," continued Kipling, "and the remainder positively pretty, would you not spend your time making love?" Despite this apparent lack of exertion, prior to the Second World War this land of plenty was the world's largest exporter of rice — three million tons annually.

This happy state of affairs existed for two reasons: a clement climate and the fertile deposits from the Irrawaddy and her tributaries. The monsoon rains sweep in from the Indian Ocean but their harshness is curbed by the wall of mountains encircling the country, especially the Arakan Yoma to the west. The "rice bowl" of Burma is the rich alluvial land of the Irrawaddy delta. This area is some 150 miles wide and 180 miles long and, it has been calculated, the deposit of silt is causing it to encroach into the Bay of Bengal at the rate of approximately three miles a century (which is hard to believe when one considers that this is the equivalent of over one yard per week). It boasts nine million acres under cultivation and alone produces enough rice to feed the population of Burma. It seems "hardly any possible number of crops in a season could apparently exhaust the fertility of the soil". Upper Burma, due to the greater mountain protection, is much drier, obliging the farmers to irrigate their land. Much of the irrigation system in this region dates from the eleventh century and the time of King Anawrahta (who was also responsible for the country's first unification and conversion to Theravada Buddhism). During a campaign in the Shan States he is said to have seen irrigation for the first time and to have realised that it represented the possibility of providing sufficient food for all (or nearly all) his subjects, and that a king who ensured that was a secure king.

The driest areas of all are the highlands which encircle and protect the country. So thick is the jungle, and so poor the soil in most of these areas, that their people (predominantly Burma's ethnic minorities) are forced to lead a nomadic existence. These hill tribes still practise the *taunggya* (slash-and-burn) method of cultivation: they will clear an area in the forest (the burnt timbers acting as fertiliser) large enough to produce a worthwhile crop for one or perhaps two years, and then move on, leaving the land to be reclaimed by the jungle. The method of clearing a hilly site provides a pertinent illustration of Burmese economy of labour coupled with ingenuity. Starting at the bottom of the slope a line of trees is notched lightly on the upper side; proceeding uphill the incision becomes deeper until at the top a line is cut right through; these then fall on their neighbours below, sending the rest down like a pack of cards.

I have never seen twentieth-century agricultural machinery in Burma — except for several hundred tractors given by Poland in the 1960s. These are now rusting from the rains as they sit unused in a compound near Rangoon's airport. When a Burman goes to his fields he harnesses his well-fed oxen or, in the delta area "more commonly the mud-loving buffalo, partly because the buffalo regards the toil as a pleasure on account of the mud", and drives his cart in a leisurely way along the track. (Sir George Scott would have us believe that, when making a wheel for his bullock-cart, the Burman "cuts it out of a solid slab of wood, leaves it square, or with imperfectly blunted corners, and trusts to time to round it for him".) The oxen are yoked to a "single barred harrow with three long teeth of acacia wood"; above the harrow is another crossbar of wood on which the ploughman stands and is pulled up and down the field whilst softly purring words of encouragement to his propellant. Come the blazing midday sun, beast and master will shelter and snooze under a spreading tamarind or gold mohur tree. The ploughing finished, the women and children transplant the iridescent rice seedlings. Here is essential Burma: a background of soft earth browns, the wooden implements, the

I have never seen twentieth-century agricultural machinery in Burma. The oxen are yoked to a "single barred harrow with three long teeth of acacia wood"; above the harrow is another crossbar of wood on which the ploughman stands and is pulled up and down the field whilst softly purring words of encouragement to his propellant.

honey-coloured skins highlighting the dazzling green rice, the noble tamarinds and the horizon punctuated by the graceful shape of a pagoda — a picture of peace and fecundity.

The arrival of October brings harvest, which is another family affair. The crop is scythed and the sheaths loaded onto a wooden cart. Threshing is accomplished in a variety of ways. Heads of grain spread on a tarmac road is a common sight, leaving the work to the wheels of passing vehicles, with a pretty girl on hand to sweep up the errant grain; or the sheaths are merely thwacked against a screen or an old oil drum. A third method is on a rather more advanced technical plane: the sheaths are laid in a circle on the ground round a pivot, to which a strong bar is attached. An ox is harnessed to the bar on which someone sits, legs outstretched, and round and round goes this curious team, crunching the grain, while others dart in and out sweeping and replacing sheaths. For winnowing, baskets of paddy are brought in a cart from the threshing floor and simply tipped onto a sloping bamboo mat; the husks separate and blow away.

Whereas in the delta region mostly rice is grown, in the rest of the country a myriad crops abound: cotton, sesame, tea, jute, sugarcane, maize and of course tobacco. (Burma, observed Kipling, "is a delightfully lazy land full of pretty girls and very bad cheroots.") This land of plenty also boasts a wealth of natural resources: jade, emeralds, sapphires, rubies as well as a variety of semi-precious stones, tungsten, silver, copper, tin, oil and Burma's second largest export after rice, teak. Most of the teak comes from the forests in the north. There, trees are felled with the help of elephants which then drag them down to the banks of the Irrawaddy. Here they are lashed together into large log rafts on which perches a hut to house the captain, who pilots the craft downstream. Some will make the full thousand-mile journey to the sawmills of Rangoon which today, as in the mid-nineteenth century, are "busy as an anthill all day long". For others their destination will be Mandalay. Here they are unlashed and then, trunk by trunk, hauled out of the river by water buffalo. These stately animals work in pairs; yoked together they drag the vast trunks onto the mud bank, the authoritative voice of their handler issuing commands the while and, with greater dexterity than their bumbling appearance suggests, they

manage to load the mud-covered objects onto aged lorries. After these exertions they flop back into the river, yoke and all, for a hard-earned wallow while awaiting their next turn.

In almost every town there is a thriving market. At dawn farmers, towels wrapped around their heads to ward off the early morning chill, start arriving, bearing vast baskets brimming with fresh produce. Considerable time and effort is spent in laying this out with each variety of merchandise in its allotted section. The resulting display provides an everyday demonstration of the style and sense of design seemingly inherent in all Burmese: a pyramid of glossy tomatoes on a flat basket, a round of green chilies with young aubergines as the centrepiece, and interspersed among these brilliant colours, the muted tones of mounds of tea, bundles of many-sized cheroots — with the occasional mauve cigar providing a diversion — and neat stacks of the cosmetic thanaka wood. Thanaka powder is popular as a cosmetic with women all over Burma for its astringent and cooling as well as its aesthetic qualities. Branches cut from the thanaka tree (linnoria acidissiura) are sold either in short lengths or in powder form, ground on a *kyankpyin*, a flat piece of stone encircled by a groove (the harder the stone the smoother the paste). The wearer applies the powder however she thinks prettiest, usually in large circles on the cheeks. Without question, Burmese maidens and matrons alike boast fine complexions. According to the Burmese writer, Mi Mi Khaing, "even the most ardent Max Factor fans cannot give up thanaka entirely for its great value lies in its astringent properties".

One's nose leads one to where fish of all shapes and sizes are laid out. Here too will be found *ngapi*, a fish paste which is a delight to the Burmese but definitely an acquired taste for the foreigner. "The smell of ngapi," remarked the by no means over-sensitive Sir George Scott, "is certainly not charming to an uneducated nose". It is a relish which can accompany any dish. There are three distinct types: *ngapi gaung*, consisting of whole fish pressed and dried and later eaten baked; *ngapi seinsa* made from the squeezed and fermented juices of shrimp, which is stored in earthenware pots, not dissimilar to anchovy paste; and thirdly and most pungent, *ngapi-yecho (taungtba)*. This is made from small fish which are left

Tobacco roasting in an enormous wok — cigars and pipe smoking begins at an early age in Burma, in many cases soon after learning to walk.

uncleaned in the sun for a day or two ("by which time their condition is better imagined than closely investigated"); then they are salted, pounded and stored in clay pots.

Fishing is one of Burma's contradictions. Buddhist philosophy says "thou shalt not take any life at all"; yet fish is a Burman's favourite food, so a compromise had to be reached — it is acceptable to buy fish and indeed meat and poultry (butchers in Burma are predominantly Muslim or Chinese) as long as one did not actually order the animal in question to be slaughtered. So where does that leave the fisherman? He is regarded by some as the lowest category of man who will undoubtedly be banished to the Bông of Animals in the next life. To others the fisherman "is nobly drawing demerit on further reincarnations by providing the nation's favourite food". And to his own conscience? Why, he is saving the fish from drowning! (He plucks the fish from the water laying them on the bank to recover, and if they die that is not his fault.) The result of this somewhat tortuous arrangement seems to be that every Burmese river is peopled with fishermen. On the bank men stand knee-deep in mud, with a cylindrical basket in which to store their catch strapped on their back. As one sails past, an object shaped like some prehistoric creature may bob to the surface: this is one of the fish traps used in deeper waters. Meanwhile, varieties of small craft move slowly across the surface of the water, a line dangling over the gunwale, the occupant perhaps dozing under his hat.

"The most calm and contented of mortals" was the nineteenth-century British view of the Burmese, and this seems true of the great majority of her people today. Burma is so generously endowed with the fruits of the earth (and of the waters) — that the early Mons bestowed on her the name Golden Land. What possible reason could there be, the Burmese seem to ask, to go about harvesting these fruits with a greater sense of urgency?

Small fish spread out on straw mats to dry, some are even tucked into hats; come sundown the fish are transferred into baskets and carried home along the soft pink sands of the Bay of Bengal.

Threshing is accomplished in a variety of ways. Heads of grain spread on a tarmac road is a common sight, leaving the work to the wheels of passing vehicles, or the sheaths are merely thwacked against a screen or an old oil drum.

One of Burma's contradictions is being played out in the evening light. Fishermen prepare to put out to sea; at the next morning's market their catch will be on sale. Fish is Burma's food, but as good Buddhists these fishermen go "to save the fish from drowning".

A Stir About of Rainbows

An ethnographical map of Burma shows a patchwork of peoples. The main group, the Burmese, live in what the British called "Burma Proper", the lowland areas along the Irrawaddy River. Of today's population of some 35 million, two-thirds are Burmans while the remaining third divide into five main minority groups and some sixty smaller ones.

There is evidence of man — though not where he had come from — inhabiting the area around the Irrawaddy valley some 5,000 years ago. Perhaps these settlements were staging posts on the main route from Assam to Indochina. Then for a time, some tribes had made coastal settlements prior to moving southeast to Indonesia. But the first permanent settlers of whom we can be certain were the Mons. They came from the east in about 200 B.C. with the expansion of the Mon-Khmer Empire (from which modern Cambodia is descended). They named the lush country they had discovered Suvannabhumi (Golden Land). Shortly afterwards, first the Pyus and then the Burmans (Mramma) fled their native southeast Tibet in the face of aggression from both the Tibetans and the Chinese. The Pyus formed the spearhead of the migration: they came to rest in the southern reaches of the Irrawaddy and founded a kingdom at Sri Ksetra, while the Burmans themselves settled in central Burma. In the seventh century the Mons, who had settled in the southeast, fought and defeated the Pyus, pushing them north where they merged with the Burmans and made their joint capital at Pagan in 849.

The peoples of these early migrations had much the same Mongolian features, "very little of the Chinese tilt of the eye", tending in skin colour to "vary from the tint of a wax candle to that of a dead oak-leaf". The Arakanese who settled in the southwest were part of this same exodus from the "vast steppes of high Asia", though by being virtually cut off from "Burma Proper" by the Arakan Yoma, their language developed differently. There is no "r" in Burmese, whereas the Arakanese not only have one but roll it with all the style of the French.

The Karens, however, are of totally different stock. It is thought they originated from the Gobi Desert, which their ancestors called the River of Sand. Their folklore contains stories of a seven-day creation, a great flood and "the names of Adam and Eve". These biblical parallels have led ethnologists to speculate that they could be one of Israel's ten lost tribes.

The final major group called the Tai-Shans came from the conquered kingdom of Nanchao. This comprised the present-day Yunnan Province of southwest China, and was a federation of tribal groups modelled on that of the neighbouring Tang regime. During the eighth and ninth centuries they had made periodic raids into Burma, attacking the Pyu kingdom. When in the thirteenth century they in turn were conquered by Kublai Khan and became a suzerain state of his empire, a vast exodus of these Tai-Shan people ensued. Many went to Thailand where they found the great cities of Chiangmai and Ayutthia. (The word "Siam" is thought to be the old French spelling of Shan which is the Burmese name for Northern Tai — free man — people.) Another major group of Tai-Shans settled in Upper Burma of which they usurped control, building their capitals first at Sagaing and then in 1364 at Ava, and extending their territory as far south as Prome. Thus the situation remained, until the Burmese unified the country (for the second time) in 1555 and the Shans resettled on the high fertile plateau to the east of Ava. In 1752 the ever turbulent Mons, who had been centred on Pegu since its founding in 825, had a final fling against Burmese supremecy; but by 1760 the Burmese had firmly reasserted their power. Ironically the achievement of the Burmese, having established control of the country after centuries of fighting, was shortlived. The long arm of the British Raj was soon to chip away their territory, and by 1885 the whole of Burma had become part of British India.

At the time of their annexation of Burma, the British felt that "the great want of the country is population". A supposed four million lived in Lower Burma and two million in Upper Burma. However, the latter figure was largely guess-work, since many of the ethnic groups had disappeared into the hills as a result of constant bullying at the hands of the corrupt regime of King Theebaw. Local government was organised in

As grandmother winds the yarn on this strange contraption the more strenuous task of weaving is carried on below. From these unlikely workshops beautiful longyis are produced.

a manner which was bound to result in oppression and inefficiency: an official was designated to administer a particular region and, after meeting the costs of doing so (which of course he kept to the minimum) was permitted to keep the lion's share of the proceeds. It was little wonder that this job bore the title Myo-Sa (Town-eater); "the more a man cultivated," it was said, "the more grievously was he squeezed".

The minority peoples adopted differing attitudes towards their Burman oppressors. The Shans attributed their position to trickery. The two groups were in conflict over a certain desirable tract of land, for which the robust Shans were prepared to fight, but the Burmese called in a hermit to arbitrate, and declared that the winner of the land would be whoever first built a pagoda on the site. In no time the physically superior Shans were in the lead. During the night the crafty Burmese erected a bamboo shell, covered it with cloth and plastered it white. The next morning the Shans were shattered to find the pagoda "completed" and even with offerings to Buddha in place, so that they "never dreamed of examining the precocious paya".

The Karens blamed the divine power for their misfortunes. The creator, they believed, threw three clods of earth on the ground: from one sprang the Burmese, from the second the Karens and the third the Kalas (foreigners). Because the Karens were so talkative, the creator threw another handful to the Burmese, thus making them supreme.

These animosities towards the Burmese, deeply ingrained in the culture of several minority peoples, help to explain why Burma has never become a totally homogeneous nation, and why today several groups are still fighting for their autonomy.

To Sir George Scott, Burmese dress in its rich variety of forms suggested "wind-stirred tulip beds or a stir about of rainbows". Of all Burma's ethnic groups the Burmese themselves are the least frivolous. Both men and women wear cotton longyis (silk for grand occasions), with neat and often white muslin blouses (eingyi) for the women and ordinary cotton shirts for the men. On special occasions, however, Burmese men don white collarless shirts under crisp cotton waist-length jackets. (I wonder if Burma is the original

home of flip-flops? In the eighteenth and nineteenth centuries they were standard footwear, and of course today everyone wears them, though often made of velvet.) Traditionally both men and women wore their hair long, coiled in a variety of styles on top of their heads, sometimes filled out by a hairpiece. The men would encircle their topknot with a scarf — one finds some older men coiffed thus today — whereas the women complete the effect with a bone comb and seasonal flowers. The maidens of Rangoon popularly believed that to sweep the western stairway of the Shwedagon Pagoda was to bring "the doer beauty of long and black hair in the next existence". The picture as a whole is truly elegant: "indeed both men and women seem incapable of making an error in taste" even to the extent of young beauties puffing away at large cigars (though "they round a young lady's mouth a little too much perhaps").

One of Burma's largest minority groups are the Shans. When in 1555 they were pushed out of Central Burma the majority resettled on a high plateau (3,200 feet above sea level), sandwiched between the Kingdoms of Ava and Thailand. Fine agriculturists that they were, the Shans were quick to make the best of its temperate climate and fertile soil. The area was divided into thirty-four princedoms, ruled by Sawbwas "who retain all the forms and appurtenances of royalty". They in turn paid tribute in varying degrees, either to the King of Ava, the Chinese Empire, Ayutthia or Vientiane, depending on proximity and the vicissitudes of local politics. Throughout the period of the British Raj this situation was allowed to continue, although the Shan States came under the nominal and relatively informal jurisdiction of a governor. The first and most famous of these was Sir George Scott (Shway Yoe), Superintendent of the Shan States, whose accounts of Burmese society and history provide a cornucopia of learning and finely observed detail. In 1947 when Independence was granted and the Constitution drawn up, the Shans, along with other ethnic groups, were persuaded with the option of their own independence in ten years, to join the Union of Burma. Until then they had retained a degree of autonomy with the Sawbwas still in charge of local government. However, after Ne Win assumed control of a caretaker government in 1958, the promise of independence

A group of Kachins who have travelled from Burma's far north to visit the Shwedagon Pagoda in Rangoon, the major Buddhist shrine.

A Palaung mother and baby epitomise Sir George Scott's remark on the varieties of Burmese dress: a "sight which is not readily forgotten, wind stirred tulip-beds, or a stir about of rainbows are the only suggestions which can be offered".

was revoked, all the Sawbwas' lands were confiscated and, after an unsuccessful independence bid, many of them were imprisoned. Today, although free, they are not allowed to return to their homeland and their activities are closely monitored. Much of the Shan States is still classified as a "brown" area (and considered unsafe for visitors) as it is controlled by Shan rebels, who have in effect become warlords. The Shan States form a large part of the notorious Golden Triangle which straddles the Burmese-Thai border. It is the growth of opium in this virtually impenetrable region that largely finances the Shans' continuing militant activity.

Of all Burma's ethnic groups only Shan men traditionally wear trousers. With more the appearance of divided skirts, these are baggy garments which hang from a wide loose waist-band folded over and tucked in, and worn with the same crisp jackets as the Burmans. The Shans also originated the rectangular fabric shoulder bag, though today these are carried by men throughout Burma. Shan men and women both use *khamouts* (elegant conical-shaped straw hats similar to those worn in Thailand) as protection against the fierce midday sun.

Three interesting groups living in Shan country, but who are of Mon-Khmer rather than Shan stock, are the Padaungs, the Palaungs and the Inthas. The Padaung womenfolk traditionally wore gold rings around their necks and ankles. From the age of six or seven a new ring was added each year, eventually stretching the neck to about 12 inches. The original purpose of this custom was to repel prospective kidnappers — though one might think these gold-encased "giraffe women" constituted a positive invitation — but the practice is now illegal for medical reasons. However, ladies of middle age are still to be seen wearing their bondage: once ringed they cannot in effect be released, for the golden corset has stretched and eventually replaced the neck muscles.

The Inthas live near Taungyi, the capital of the Shan States (founded by Sir George Scott), on the breathtakingly beautiful Inle Lake. Not far away, around Kalaw (a favourite hill station retreat of the colonials, and still a little England of stockbroker Tudor houses surrounded by aster- and snapdragon-filled gardens), are the various Palaung settlements. The Palaung womenfolk are positive birds of

paradise against the restful greens of their mountain jungle landscape, and the drab browns of their smoky villages. An unmarried girl might wear a thick red striped longyi with an embroidered green velvet jacket, a cotton tasselled "halo" perched on her long shiny black hair. Her longyi is not tucked in like a Burman's but held in place by a wide white belt. For a working day the velvet jacket is replaced by an embroidered cotton one sightly faded from constant washing and the sun, and the halo discarded in favour of a band around her forehead suppporting the weight of a produce-laden basket on her back. When she marries she can substitute a blue or purple jacket with red facing; around her waist hangs a collection of thin lacquer bands and her head is encased by cotton strands from which at the back dangle silver beads — a stunning ensemble worn with great panache. The Palaungs' predominant crop is tea which they sell "in the form of hard balls rather larger than cricket balls"; they are also famous for their lapet. Before roads reached their remote villages, the lapet was carried over the hills to the Irrawaddy where the baskets were strapped to rafts and floated down river semi-submerged.

The other major rebel army, other than the Shans, is that of the Karens — the Karen National Liberation Army. The predominantly Christian Karens are excellent soldiers, and during colonial times were widely recruited and promoted within the British Army, some acquiring Sandhurst training in the process. Like the Shans, the Karens also felt they had been unfairly treated as a result of the 1947 Constitution. The Liberation Army, scattered in pockets along Burma's south-east border with Thailand and in the Irrawaddy delta region, lives on, largely financed by the lucrative smuggling trade.

Both the Kachins, who inhabit the mountainous regions in the north of Burma, and the Chins whose home is to the west of the country, also provided a plentiful source of soldiery for the British. Many Kachins were trained by the American O.S.S. during World War II in the fight against the Japanese. The Kachin national dress in particular is another eye-catcher: red calf-length longyis worn over tight trousers and black velvet jackets decorated with silver bangles. The men, in their dark longyis and blue jackets, carry silver-decorated shoulder bags and elegantly curved silver swords and scabbards.

Geographically, both the Chins and their southerly neighbours, the Arakanese, have been cut off from Burma Proper more than the other minority groups. On the one hand, the Arakanese were able to retain their autonomy over centuries by standing up for themselves — they sacked the Burmese capital on several occasions. The Chins on the other hand were content to keep to their hills. Today, the Burmese remain suspicious of the Arakanese and warn prospective visitors to take care!

Despite the diversity and geographic separation of Burma's ethnic "wind-stirred tulip bed", these peoples share with each other and with the Burmans themselves a wide variety of social customs — the longyi, thanaka cosmetics, betel and lapet are to be found throughout Burma. Pay a call on a Burmese family, whether as a friend or a total stranger, and you will first be offered tea and then betel and lapet. Both delicacies are stored in partitioned boxes of either lacquer or silver. In the betel box the top layer will house orange peel, lime and chopped areca nut with fresh betel leaves underneath. Select your leaf, spread it with the nuts, lime and peel and chew it, spitting out the strong red juice. The taste is pungent — said to aid the digestion — and leaves the novice a little numb in the mouth and light in the head. Lapet is also a mild stimulant but with culinary distinction, "it clears the palate into sweetness". Young tea leaves are pressed in bamboo containers and stored in a moist atmosphere which gently ferments them. Before serving, they are mixed with a little sesame oil and salt and eaten with morsels of dried shrimps, roasted peanuts, fried crispy garlic and broad beans. "Students apt to doze over exam books pause, not to take a pill but to make lapet salad and keep awake on its pep."

Another quality which Burma's minority groups share is expertise in weaving. Very often the womenfolk of the village will form a weaving guild, each area producing indigenous fabric. In more primitive villages it is common to hear the clack of the loom coming from under the house, in the cowshed. The craftswoman sits on the earthern floor, her outstretched legs resting against a bamboo pole, her work suspended from an H-shape frame and held taut by a strap going around her waist.

The Kachins and Chins, inhabiting the lower lying and relatively fertile hills in Burma's south and west, have been able to develop settled village societies based on a self-sustaining crop rotation system of agriculture. However, most of Burma's hill tribes still depend on the taunggya (slash-and-burn) method of cultivation for obtaining the fruits of the soil. Every few years, having exhausted the goodness of the land they have cleared from the jungle, the whole village moves on. Choosing a new site is obviously of critical importance: the traditional method of doing this (and who can be sure it is not practised today?) has a specially Burmese otherworldly quality. Each householder would go out to select a favourite site and from it bring home a clod of earth. That night he places it under his pillow and awaits an auspicious dream. The following day the village soothsayer analyses the dreams. If there is no outright dream winner, a large fowl is cooked and eaten by the householders and the clean bones are put in an earthenware pot. The participants, with eyes averted, each pick out a bone and the one to pick the largest has the honour of leading the village to its new home.

The Palaung womenfolk are
positive birds of paradise against
the restful greens of their
mountain jungle landscape.

92

"By some uncanny conspiracy everyday incidents become glimpses of unconscious grace and style".

93

Opposite *Karen maidens,
wearing Burmese court dress,
are each coiffed in a traditional
hairstyle.*

*Though the process used to dye
yarn is old fashioned — the
wok's temperature regulated by
a sensitive toe — the dyes are in
fact synthetic.*

Sons of the Lake

HIGH on the Shan Plateau sparkles the Inle Lake — a place of dazzling beauty and possessed of its own separate, magic quality. It is inhabited — literally, since their homes float upon the lake — by the Intha People. These people, who are of Mon rather than Shan descent, originated from the southeast of Burma around Tavoy. When or why the migration took place is unclear. Some say it was during the reign of King Narapati Tseotho (1157 to 1190 or maybe a century later!). A wealth of stories surrounds this King. He was thought to have travelled to Tavoy on a religious mission, and there he founded a city; he is also alleged to have repulsed a vast invading Chinese Army in the Inle Lake valley. Today, on the bed of the lake are rows of posts, supposedly pillars of his palace. Another theory suggests that the Inthas were convicts expelled from Tavoy in the seventeenth century; and still another that they simply became wearied with the constant battling between the Mons and Burmese. In any event the Inthas (literally meaning Sons of the Lake) not only survived in their remote mountain environment but prospered: the lake (14 miles long and, at its widest, just three miles across) now has sixty-four villages with approximately 35,000 people all living on floating islands of vegetation.

The lake reveals itself to the visitor slowly. One approaches along narrow streams hedged with high rushes, probably aboard a long canoe propelled by a lusty outboard, which whisks along at terrifying speed. Occasionally, in order to avoid another craft travelling at a more leisurely pace, one veers into the undergrowth, leaping knotted tangles of water hyacinths. Once through this maze of channels one emerges into a more tranquil world onto the mirror of water, its glassy blue reflecting the occasional cloud. To left and right the picture is framed by serried green mountains with the centre a continuous blue. Other than the growl of canoe buses as they whip to and fro, the stillness and silence are only disturbed by fishermen. They have evolved an eccentric method of rowing and fishing, specially suited to local conditions (the water being both shallow — from three to ten feet in depth — and very clear). By propelling their craft from the bow they are forewarned of approaching patches of tangled weed and, more important, are able to watch for giveaway bubbles and then pounce. With only one limb engaged in providing locomotion the rest of the body is free for the business at hand: down goes the conical-shaped net pushed home with the fisherman's leg.

Soon, one comes upon "the singular spectacle of a multitude of floating islands", consisting of row upon row of floating gardens bursting with an abundance of flowers and vegetables. These have been gradually built up over the years by cutting strips of dense weed from the lake floor. The tangled mass is consolidated with earth and eventually forms one of the most abundant growing media imaginable. New areas are constantly being "grown" in shallow water: grass cuttings and weed form the foundation, then comes a layer of earth and finally top soil. When the layers of weed and earth have become integrated, strips some six feet wide and perhaps as long as 100 yards are cut loose and poled to their destinations, where they are pegged to the lake floor with long bamboo staves.

The lake's largest village is Yamaw, its streets a web of canals, each piece of "land" connected by arched wooden bridges and causeways. One Mr Richardson (an early nineteenth-century visitor to the lake) suggested that the islands "undulate at every step, and a man's house sometimes, during a squall, changes front to every point of the compass". If this was ever the case, it certainly is not today and the ground feels quite solid underfoot. This is a rich community, and teak houses are generally handsome two-storeyed affairs. They are constructed on large wooden piles driven directly into the lake's bed, the space below the first floor being used as a boathouse. Each dwelling has its own landing stage, often no more than a floating pavement of grass, pegged by bamboo (which doubles as a bollard for visiting craft). On the plot surrounding the house are the trappings of domestic life: a tidy vegetable patch, a water pen for ducks, washing hung to dry. At one end of the plot a small area of canal, the size of a generous shower bowl, will

The moment the fisherman spies the bubbles he plunges his conical shaped net into the water, pushing it home with his leg. He then attempts to spear the ensnared fish.

be encircled by a bamboo fence; this is the scene of the family's daily washing ritual. It contains wooden planks both for sitting on as well as for use as a scrubbing board, and a large bowl for the rinsing douche, though for the younger members a splash in the canal is preferred. The Burmese are insatiable washers, both of themselves and of their clothes, and true to Burma's liberated lifestyle the men do their own laundry. From the back door of the house a walkway leads to an elevated lavatory. Despite the absence of plumbing per se, the problem is mysteriously disposed of and the air is purity and fragrance itself. Apparently even the dead are buried in the lake.

A pivot of social life is the morning's floating market which congregates on Yamaw's broadest canal, alongside the village store and nat shrines. Here, under the protective shade of their straw khamouts chattering businesswomen manoeuvre elegant canoes filled with all manner of produce. The Inthas' wealth is derived not only from their market gardening activities but also from lucrative craft industries, notably weaving of Shan shoulder bags, beautiful thick Shan longyis as well as fine and delicate silverware. Industrial methods, however, tend towards the quaint to say the least. The blacksmith's bellows operator — his grandmother — sits perched on a small platform behind two long thick bamboo tubes, alternately pulling in and out long feather dusters, causing a very effective air draft.

The lake is as richly endowed with pagodas and monasteries as anywhere else in Burma. In particular, the Phaung Daw U Pagoda is regarded (with the Shwedagon in Rangoon and the Shwezigon in Pagan) as one of the three principal shrines of Burma. This pagoda houses five small Buddha images, whose shape has long since been lost under years of plastering with gold leaf by pilgrims. Once a year at the October full moon there is an elaborate festival, during which the Buddha images are rowed around the lake to visit outlying pagodas. They are conveyed in a magnificent copy of a royal Karaweik barge shaped like a golden swan (symbol of Buddhist royalty). The minute Buddhas sit under white umbrellas of royalty. Nowadays only four of the Buddhas make this regal progress; some years ago the barge capsized with all five aboard. Their distraught guardians were only able

to recover four images but on returning to the pagoda, found the fifth miraculously in its normal position! It has not been moved since and now guards the pagoda during the others' annual outing.

Top *When the business of creating the floating vegetation is complete, the strip six feet wide and perhaps 100 yards or so long, is cut loose and poled to its destination where it will be pegged to the lake floor with long bamboo staves.* Bottom *A pivot of social life is the morning floating market which congregates on Yamaw's broadest canal alongside the village store and nat shrines.*

The ancient craft of lacquerware flourishes: "the supreme test of excellence is when the sides will bend in till they touch without cracking". Here an old man takes a rest from making monks' begging bowls.

Because the Inle Lake is both shallow — from three to ten feet — and very clear, the Intha people have evolved an eccentric method of rowing and fishing. Balancing on one leg as if in preparation for a pirouette, they tuck the oar under the other one to row. This enables the fisherman from his vantage point on the bow to watch both for approaching patches of tangled weed and also for tell-tale bubbles.

Right *A poetic environment in which to do one's washing.*
Bottom left *Bridges reminiscent of French Impressionist paintings link floating islands to one another.* Bottom right *The four minute Buddha images sit under the white umbrellas of royalty. Originally all five Buddhas from the Phaung Daw U Pagoda made this regal journey; but some years ago the Karaweik capsized and only four were recovered from the lake. On returning to the Pagoda the fifth was found miraculously in situ.*

The Middle Way

So what, if anything, is one to conclude regarding this curious country? Perhaps, Burmese style, one should not insist on neat cut-and-dried answers and be content merely to contemplate the problem standing before the quizzical gaze of the Buddha.

I would like to suggest, however, that it is in the very philosophy of Buddhism that one can find at least an approach to the question. The aura of Buddhism permeates the whole of Burmese life; certainly not limited to practising Buddhists alone, it seems to cast its spell even over the behaviour of visiting foreigners. A cardinal concept in this philosophy is that of the Middle Way — put most simply, the avoidance of extremes, the cultivation of tranquillity, the acceptance of Karma.

Denied access until recently to practically everything foreign, the Burmese have developed a genius for adaptation — a nut and bolt sticking out near the end of a strip of wood becomes a most effective bottle opener; children at play tug on a length of rope hanging through the floor of the verandah above as they dash past, thus keeping in motion the crib on the verandah and its occupant content; oil drums become fencing; contraptions apparently straight from the pages of *Charlie and the Chocolate Factory* turn out to be functioning farm implements; Willy's jeeps of 1940s vintage are kept alive by methods Western mechanics would refuse to believe. The Burmese ingenuity for improvisation, to make do with what little is at their disposal, is a source of enduring fascination. It is also an expression of the Middle Way in practice: picking one's way round a problem and arriving at a solution which, even if unexpected, satisfies all concerned. Of course, it is this same process that allows fishermen to carry out their work on the basis that they are saving their catch from drowning.

Another manifestation of the Middle Way is the serenity that it has conferred on the Burmese in almost every aspect of their daily life. The older monks, in particular, positively radiate spiritual calm. As Mi Mi Khaing observes, "there is a look of repose which they wear easily after years of daily meditation and freedom from petty irritations". This same force seems to affect the population as a whole: there is a compelling sense of man existing in harmony with his environment. By some uncanny conspiracy everyday incidents become glimpses of unconscious grace and style; a monk can stroll out into the sun and his parasol transforms into an orange halo; at dusk a bullock-cart, "a poem in curves of wood", creaks across the pink sand of the Irrawaddy; a longyi-clad girl, silhouetted, glides down a dusty avenue of tamarind trees; a motionless figure kneels in the precinct of a great pagoda, the last rays of the sun bathing its golden spire, while the bells of its hti "are moved by the wind to give sweet testimony to all spirits, and give the praying devotee a tinkling reassurance of his merit".

This to me is Burma — a land of untroubled acceptance of one's fate, of polite disinterest in the outside world, of making do; a land where most strive for oneness with Buddha, and actually achieve it with their own environment, where, in their softness and fluidity even the colours and contours of the countryside conform to the ideals of the Middle Way; a land, to give Rudyard Kipling the last word, where "they exist beautifully".

"Age is highly respected in Burma". The elderly continue to live in the family unit contributing their wisdom and guiding the family's path along the Middle Way.

"It is the timelessness which is the essence of Burma"; muted colours, beautiful trees, contented animals, boats gently moving across the water. "I know no other land where the eye is so constantly delighted by scenes of casual, almost unintended, beauty".

104

Historical-Cultural Chronology Chart

	Asia	Burma	Europe and the Western World
BC 3500	Earliest Chinese town; Long Shan culture		Invention of wheel and plough (Mesopotamia) and sail (Egypt)
3000	Use of bronze in Thailand		
2500	Growth of civilisation in the Indus valley (c.2750)	Legendary lists of Kings of Arakan begins (c.2666)	Old Kingdom, or Pyramid Age, of Egypt begins (c.2685 to 2180 B.C.)
1500	First urban civilisation in China; Shang Bronze Age culture (c.1600) Evidence of writing in China (c.1500) Development of Brahma worship in India. Composition of Vedas begins (c.1450)		Beginnings of Mycenaean civilisation in Greece (c.1600)
750	Sanskrit religious treaties (c.800-400)		Homer's *Iliad* and Hesiod's poetry first recorded (c.750)
500	Death of Siddhartha Gautama, founder of Buddhism (c.486) Death of Confucius (c.479)	First mention of a Burmese capital city (c.500) Foundation of Shwedagon Pagoda (c.480)	Period of Greek classical culture (c.479-338)
300	Ashokda, Mauryan emperor (273-236) converted to Buddhism (c.262) Shi Huang Di of Qin Dynasty unites China (221) Construction of the Great Wall		Alexander the Great invades Asia Minor, then reaches India (329)
100	Opening of Silk Road across Central Asia. Trade with Rome (c.112)	Visit of Zhang Qian, emissary from Han China (c.128)	
AD 50			Jesus of Nazareth crucified in Jerusalem (c.30) Roman invasion of Britain (43)
100		Founding of Pagan (c.108)	
150	Buddhism reaches China. Chinese Buddhist monks make pilgrimages to India		
200		Mahamuni Buddha probably cast in Arakan	
300	Founding of Constantinople (330)		Huns, Visigoths, Vandals ravage western Europe (c.370-410)
500			Death of St. Benedict (543)
600	Death of Muhammed (632)		
700	Printing in China (c.730) Paper making spreads from China to Muslim world and eventually Europe in 1150		
800			Charlemagne crowned emperor in Rome
1000	Moveable type printing invented in China (1045)	Anawrahta succeeds to throne of Pagan (1044) Establishment of first Burmese national state at Pagan (1057)	Norman conquest of Britain (1066)
1100	Angkor Empire (Cambodia) at greatest extent (c.1180)		*The Song of Roland* (c.1100)
1200	Mongols under Genghis Khan begin conquest of Asia (1206) Emergence of first Thai kingdom (c.1220) Kublai Khan founds Yuan Dynasty in China (1279)	Mongols invade Burma ending First Burmese Empire (1287) Mons establish Talaing Empire at Martaban (1287)	Magna Carta: King John makes concessions to English barons (1215) Death of St. Francis of Assisi (1226)
1300	Ming Dynasty founded in China (1368)	Sagaing founded as capital of independent Shan kingdom (1315)	Black Death from Asia invades Europe (1348)

	Asia	Burma	Europe and the Western World
1400	Vasco de Gama: first European sea voyage to India and back (1498)	New Shan Dynasty (Thedo Minya) establishes capital at Ava (1364) This dynasty of 17 kings survives until 1554	Columbus reaches America (1492)
1500	Babus conquers Kingdom of Delhi and founds Mughal Dynasty (1526)	Portuguese establish trade ports in Arakan and Syriam (1519) Second Burmese Empire established at Pegu (1541) King Bayinnaung expands empire to include Chiangmai and Ayutthia (1550-81) First British trader (Ralph Fitch) visits Burma (1586)	Italian Renaissance Tobacco first introduced to Europe (1559)
1600	Manchus found Qing Dynasty in China (1644) Taj Mahal at Agra completed (1653)	Felipe de Brito impaled in Syriam after 13 years as Governor (1613)	Foundation of British and Dutch East India Companies Puritans land in New England (1620) English Civil War begins (1642)
1700	Foundation of Calcutta by English (1690)		New Amsterdam taken by British from Dutch (later renamed New York) (1664) French Revolution begins (1789)
	Greatest extent of China's empire, under Emperor Qian Long	King Alaungpaya founds Third Burmese Empire (1755) King Alaungpaya founds Rangoon (1760)	
1810		King Alaungpaya sacks Ayutthia, conquers Arakan and moves capital to Amarapoura (1760)	George Washington becomes first President of U.S.A. (1789)
1820	Britain defeats Marathas and becomes effective ruler of India (1818) British found Singapore as free trade port (1819)		Napolean defeated at Waterloo (1815)
		Burmese invade British India (1824)	First passenger steam train, Stockton to Darlington (England) (1825)
1830 1840		First Anglo-Burmese War. Assam, Arakan and Tenasserim annexed by Britain (1824-26)	
1850		Treaty of Yandabo (1825)	First electric telegraph (Britain) (1838) *Communist Manifesto* issued by Marx and Engels (1848)
	Opium War. Britain annexes Hong Kong (1842) Taiping Rebellion in China (1850-64)	Second Anglo-Burmese War. Lower Burma annexed (1852)	Darwin publishes *The Origin of Species* (1859)
	Indian Mutiny (1857)	King Mindon comes to throne of Ava (1853) King Mindon builds Gem City of Mandalay (1857)	
1860	End of Tokugawa Shogunate in Japan (1868)		American Civil War. Slavery abolished in U.S.A. (1861-5) Emancipation of Russian serfs (1861) Suez Canal opens (1869)
1870		Burmese mission to Europe; received by Queen Victoria (1872) Fifth Buddhist Synod in Mandalay (1871-2) King Mindon dies. King Theebaw succeeds (1878) Members of royal family murdered (1879)	Emergence of Impressionist school of painting (1874)

	Asia	Burma	Europe and the Western World
1880		King Theebaw negotiates treaty with the French (1884) Third Anglo-Burmese War (1885-6) Formal annexation. Burma becomes a province of British India (1886) King Theebaw exiled to Calcutta (1886)	
1890	Sino-Japanese War. Japan occupies Formosa (1894-5)		Boer War begins (1899)
1900	Boxer Uprising in China		
1910	Chinese Republican Revolution: Sun Yat-sen first President (1911)		Outbreak of First World War (1914)
			Russian Revolution (1917) League of Nations established (1919)
1920	Gandhi's non-cooperation movement in India (1921-2)	Montagu—Chelmsford reforms in India (Dyarchy) extended to Burma (1922)	Wall Street stock market crash (1929)
1930		Burma separated from British India and given Legislative Council (1937)	Outbreak of Second World War (1939)
1940	Japan attacks U.S.A. at Pearl Harbour (1941)	Japan invades Lower Burma (1941)	Development of penicillin (1939) Defeat of Germany and end of Second World War (1945)
	Civil war in China (1946)	The Burmese government together with Aung San's Liberation Army declare Burma independent (1943)	
	India and Pakistan become independent nations (1947) Communists come to power in China (1949)	Rangoon recaptured. Japanese surrender (1945) Union of Burma becomes independent. Thakis Nu Prime Minister (1948)	
1950	Bandung Conference of Third World leaders (1954)	Sixth Buddhist Synod held in Rangoon (1954-6) Ne Win heads caretaker government (1958)	Fifth Republic in France. De Gaulle first President (1958)
1960	Escalation of U.S. involvement in Vietnam War (1964) Cultural Revolution in China (1966)	Thakis Nu regains power in elections (1960) Ne Win heads successful military coup (1962)	East Germans build the Berlin Wall (1961) Cuban missile crisis (1962)
1970	Vietnam unified under the communists (1975) Death of Mao Tse-tung and fall of Gang of Four in China (1976) Death and tragedy in Cambodia (1977) USSR invades Afghanistan (1979)	Socialist Republic of the Union of Burma created (1974) Major earthquake in Pagan (1975)	First man on the moon (1969) President Nixon resigns following Watergate Affair (1974) Egypt and Israel sign peace treaty at White House (1979)
1980	Discussions between Britain and China on the future of Hong Kong (1983)	Ne Win retires from Presidency but retains Chairmanship of the Burma Socialist Program Party (1981)	Debates on nuclear disarmament

Suggested Reading

Many of the empire builders and adventurers, priests and merchants, and other motley travellers that Burma has attracted have written about the country, often with style, perception and not infrequently, wit.

As in the case of India, colonialists (disciplined, enquiring, keen-eyed types) have provided some of the most useful as well as enjoyable accounts. Two such were Sir Henry Yule and Sir George Scott — both quintessential men of the Victorian Raj — whose works I have quoted extensively and drawn upon for much contemporary data. Yule, who joined the Bengal Engineers in 1840, travelled to Burma as secretary to Colonel Arthur Phayre's mission to Ava in 1855. His 380-page *A Narrative of the Mission to the Court of Ava in 1855* (Captain Henry Yule, London: Smith, Elder, and Co. 1858. Oxford in Asia Historical Reprints, Oxford University Press 1968) both chronicles the Mission voyage up the Irrawaddy to the Court of King Mindon and also provides a penetrating social study. The facsimile edition has an informative introduction by Professor Hugh Tinker. The copious and often beautiful illustrations include drawings and watercolours by the mission's official artist, Colesworthy Grant, as well as by the author, helpful maps and also photographs by the unforgettable Linneus Tripe — a positive cornucopia of a book.

Sir George Scott joined the Burma Commission in 1886 and proceeded to build an immensely distinguished career, notably as Superintendent for the Northern and later Southern Shan States. Shway Yoe (Subject of the Great Queen), as he became entitled, earned widespread affection and respect amongst the Burmese. He wrote prolifically and also with great insight and sensitivity about the country and its people. In particular *The Burman, His Life and Notions* (Macmillan and Sons 1910) and *Burma as it was, as it is and as it will be* (George Redway 1886) remain, with minor exceptions, accurate descriptions of daily life, a century after they were written.

In the late nineteenth century, the ship on which Rudyard Kipling was travelling made a brief stop in Rangoon and then in Moulmein. This short interlude he records in Volume I of *From Sea to Sea* (1899 Doubleday McClure, New York and 1900 Macmillan, London); in these few days he managed to imbibe the feel and beauty of the country and its occupants. Burma also features in several of his poems and the much quoted "Mandalay" is most conveniently found in the *Oxford Dictionary of Quotations* (Oxford University Press, Third Edition 1979).

The historian and novelist, Maurice Collis, had in the 1920s been a member of the Indian Civil Service stationed near Mandalay in Sagaing and later in Rangoon. His *Land of the Great Image* (Faber 1942) tells the remarkable tale of the Portuguese Jesuit Father Manrique's journey to, and three years' sojourn at the Arakan capital of Myohaung in the 1620s.

Of his many other books on Burma I found *Siamese White* and *Trials in Burma* (Faber 1938) the most interesting.

George Orwell was another English novelist who found himself stationed in Burma in the 1920s. He portrays the stilted Raj life in *Burmese Days* (Penguin 1982) with acid disdain. His subsequent short stories on Burma, *A Hanging* in *Decline of the English Murder* (Penguin 1983) and *Shooting an Elephant* in *Inside the Whale* (Penguin 1982), are particularly moving.

Perhaps the best English novel set in Burma is F. Tennyson-Jesse's *The Lacquer Lady* (reprint, Virago 1979), a beautifully written and spellbinding reconstruction of the extraordinary true story of Fanny Moroni at the court of King Theebaw and Queen Supyalat, and how her love affair literally precipitated annexation of Mandalay and Northern Burma by the British. Miss Tennyson-Jesse's *The Story of Burma* (Macmillan and Sons 1946), though lacking the surrealist romance of *The Lacquer Lady*, is nevertheless an excellent historical study of Burma up to the Second World War. (Written while the Japanese were still in occupation, the final chapter asks "What next?".)

E.C.V. Foucar lived in Burma as a child and later, until the Japanese invasion in 1942, as a barrister. Of his extensive writings about the country, *Mandalay the Golden* (Dobson 1963) is perhaps his most lively. He paints a vivid picture of "the fabled city where torture and sudden death were meted out" mainly at the instigation of the bloodthirsty and implacable Queen Supyalat (inevitably nicknamed "soup plate" by the British troops).

As for pure history books, those I found the most helpful and interesting include *The Pagoda War* by A.T.Q. Stewart (Faber 1972) which deals with the Anglo-Burmese conflicts of the mid-nineteenth century; *Stilwell and the American Experience in China* by Barbara Tuchman (Macmillan 1971); *The Making of Burma* by Dorothy Woodman (Cresset Press 1962); *The Stricken Peacock* by the Burmese historian, Maung Htin Aung (Martinus Nijhoff 1965); and *A History of Modern Burma* by J.F. Cady (Cornell University Press 1958).

Two books which afford the reader a unique insight into Burmese family life and philosophy are by the renowned Burmese authoress Mi Mi Khaing. The first *The Burmese Family* (Longmans 1946) is dedicated to her "Father and mother" who have "shown to five children the shining path of moderation that is the Middle Way", so through her sensitive and lyrical prose Daw Mi Mi Khaing reveals the path of the Middle Way to the reader. In the second book *Cook and Entertain the Burmese Way* (Daw Ma Ma Khin 1975, available in Burma) the secrets of the Burmese housewife are vouchsafed. Daw Mi Mi Khaing, a university lecturer, is at present finishing a book on the role of women in Burmese society.

There are presently available two English-language guide books dealing with the country as a whole: *Burma: a travel survival kit* (Lonely Planet 1979), and the *Insight Guide to Burma* (Apa Productions 1981). The latter's comprehensive coverage and excellent photographs more than compensate for occasional inaccuracies. Several interesting books for the traveller are published in Burma. Among those I have found helpful are *Pictorial Guide to Pagan* compiled by the Director of Burma's Archaeological Survey; *The Golden Glory: Shwedagon Pagoda* compiled by the Directorate of Information; and *Historical Sites in Burma* by Aung Thau. Finally, there are Dr Htin Aung's excellent handbooks which help one get under the skin of Burmese culture. Some of these have recently been republished in Burma including *Burmese Law Tales*, *Burmese Folk Tales*, *Burmese Drama*, *and Folk Elements in Burmese Buddhism*.

An actress prepares for an evening pwè, her dressing room a cart.

Festivals

Burmese Lunar Calendar

Tagu	March/April
Kason	April/May
Nayon	May/June
Waso	June/July
Wagaung	July/August
Tawthalin	August/September
Thadingyut	September/October
Tazaungmon	October/November
Nadaw	November/December
Pyatho	December/January
Tabodwe	January/February
Taboung	February/March

Major Festivals

March/April (Tagu)
Tagu is the month when Thingyau, the Water Festival, is celebrated. It marks the visit to earth of Thagymin — King of the Nats — and the start of the Burmese New Year.

April/May (Kason)
At the full moon the birth, enlightenment and attainment of Nirvana of the Gautama Buddha is celebrated.

June/July (Waso)
The full moon heralds the start of the three-month Buddhist Lent.

August/September (Tawthalin)
This is the month of boat races, including the lavish festival on the Inle Lake.

September/October (Thadingyut)
The full moon of Thadingyut marks the end of Buddhist Lent and the Gautama Buddha's return to earth. His return is celebrated by the Festival of Light. For three days Burma is illuminated by millions of candles and lamps and a festive air abounds.

October/November (Tazaungmon)
During Tazaungmon the Weaving Festival is held. Throughout the night of the full moon the clack-clack from the looms of unmarried girls reverberates around pagoda precincts. They are competing to weave new robes for the monks. If in Burma during this festival, try and visit the Shwedagon Pagoda where the beauty and romance of this scene is paramount.

November/December (Nadaw)
Nadaw is the month of Nat Festivals.

December/January (Pyatho)
During Pyatho the majority of local pagoda festivals is celebrated.

January/February (Tabodwe)
Tobodwe is the time of the Harvest Festival (Htamane).

Glossary

daw	title of respect for an older woman
hti	golden umbrella at the summit of a pagoda
Karma	a person's fate due to his actions in a previous incarnation
khamout	conical shaped hat worn by the Shans
kyaung	Buddhist monastery
lapet	pickled tea leaf
longyi	sarong worn by both sexes
mohingha	Burmese breakfast of noodles and soup
nat	spirit
ngapi	paste made from prawns
Nirvana	the "timeless state of bliss"
pwè	an entertainment
pyongyi	Buddhist monk
shin-pyu	initiation ceremony into the monkhood for boys
shwe	gold, golden
thanaka	tree whose bark is ground into a cosmetic
u	title of respect for an older man
viss	unit of measure, equal to approximately 4½ ounces

Transliteration from the Burmese does not conform to a single system; one comes across the same word spelt a multitude of different ways. For the avoidance of confusion I have tried to be consistent in the spelling.

Index